COMMON CORE MATHEMATICS

NEW YORK EDITION

A Story of Units

Grade 2, Module 5: Addition and Subtraction Within 1,000 with Word Problems to 100

COMMON CORE™ *consider the source*

JB JOSSEY-BASS™

A Wiley Brand

Cover design by Chris Clary

Published by Jossey-Bass
A Wiley Brand
One Montgomery Street, Suite 1200, San Francisco, CA 94104-4594—www.josseybass.com

ISBN: 978-1-118-81122-1

Printed in the United States of America
FIRST EDITION
PB Printing   10 9 8 7 6 5 4 3 2 1

WELCOME

Dear Teacher,

Thank you for your interest in Common Core's curriculum in mathematics. Common Core is a non-profit organization based in Washington, DC dedicated to helping K-12 public schoolteachers use the power of high-quality content to improve instruction.[1] We are led by a board of master teachers, scholars, and current and former school, district, and state education leaders. Common Core has responded to the Common Core State Standards' (CCSS) call for "content-rich curriculum"[2] by creating new, CCSS-based curriculum materials in mathematics, English Language Arts, history, and (soon) the arts. All of our materials are written by teachers who are among the nation's foremost experts on the new standards.

In 2012 Common Core won three contracts from the New York State Education Department to create a PreKindergarten–12th grade mathematics curriculum for the teachers of that state, and to conduct associated professional development. The book you hold contains a portion of that work. In order to respond to demand in New York and elsewhere, modules of the curriculum will continue to be published, on a rolling basis, as they are completed. This curriculum is based on New York's version of the CCSS (the CCLS, or Common Core Learning Standards). Common Core will be releasing an enhanced version of the curriculum this summer on our website, commoncore.org. That version also will be published by Jossey-Bass, a Wiley brand.

Common Core's curriculum materials are not merely aligned to the new standards, they take the CCSS as their very foundation. Our work in math takes its shape from the expectations embedded in the new standards—including the instructional shifts and mathematical progressions, and the new expectations for student fluency, deep conceptual understanding, and application to real-life context. Similarly, our ELA and history curricula are deeply informed by the CCSS's new emphasis on close reading, increased use of informational text, and evidence-based writing.

Our curriculum is distinguished not only by its adherence to the CCSS. The math curriculum is based on a theory of teaching math that is proven to work. That theory posits that mathematical knowledge is most coherently and

---

1. Despite the coincidence of name, Common Core and the Common Core State Standards are not affiliated. Common Core was established in 2007, prior to the start of the Common Core State Standards Initiative, which was led by the National Governors Association and the Council for Chief State School Officers.

2. *Common Core State Standards for English Language Arts & Literacy in History/Social Studies, Science, and Technical Subjects* (Washington, DC: Common Core State Standards Initiative), 6.

effectively conveyed when it is taught in a sequence that follows the "story" of mathematics itself. This is why we call the elementary portion of this curriculum "A Story of Units," to be followed by "A Story of Ratios" in middle school, and "A Story of Functions" in high school. Mathematical concepts flow logically, from one to the next, in this curriculum. The sequencing has been joined with methods of instruction that have been proven to work, in this nation and abroad. These methods drive student understanding beyond process, to deep mastery of mathematical concepts. The goal of the curriculum is to produce students who are not merely literate, but fluent, in mathematics.

It is important to note that, as extensive as these curriculum materials are, they are not meant to be prescriptive. Rather, they are intended to provide a basis for teachers to hone their own craft through study, collaboration, training, and the application of their own expertise as professionals. At Common Core we believe deeply in the ability of teachers and in their central and irreplaceable role in shaping the classroom experience. We strive only to support and facilitate their important work.

The teachers and scholars who wrote these materials are listed beginning on the next page. Their deep knowledge of mathematics, of the CCSS, and of what works in classrooms defined this work in every respect. I would like to thank Louisiana State University professor of mathematics Scott Baldridge for the intellectual leadership he provides to this project. Teacher, trainer, and writer Robin Ramos is the most inspired math educator I've ever encountered. It is Robin and Scott's aspirations for what mathematics education in America *should* look like that is spelled out in these pages.

Finally, this work owes a debt to project director Nell McAnelly that is so deep I'm confident it never can be repaid. Nell, who leads LSU's Gordon A. Cain Center for STEM Literacy, oversees all aspects of our work for NYSED. She has spent days, nights, weekends, and many cancelled vacations toiling in her efforts to make it possible for this talented group of teacher-writers to produce their best work against impossible deadlines. I'm confident that in the years to come Scott, Robin, and Nell will be among those who will deserve to be credited with putting math instruction in our nation back on track.

Thank you for taking an interest in our work. Please join us at www.commoncore.org.

Lynne Munson
President and Executive Director
Common Core
Washington, DC
October 25, 2013

Common Core's K-5 Math Staff

Scott Baldridge, Lead Mathematician and Writer
Robin Ramos, Lead Writer, PreKindergarten-5
Jill Diniz, Lead Writer, 6-12
Ben McCarty, Mathematician

Nell McAnelly, Project Director
Tiah Alphonso, Associate Director
Jennifer Loftin, Associate Director
Catriona Anderson, Curriculum Manager,
    PreKindergarten-5

Sherri Adler, PreKindergarten
Debbie Andorka-Aceves, PreKindergarten

Kate McGill Austin, Kindergarten
Nancy Diorio, Kindergarten
Lacy Endo-Peery, Kindergarten
Melanie Gutierrez, Kindergarten
Nuhad Jamal, Kindergarten
Cecilia Rudzitis, Kindergarten
Shelly Snow, Kindergarten

Beth Barnes, First Grade
Lily Cavanaugh, First Grade
Ana Estela, First Grade
Kelley Isinger, First Grade
Kelly Spinks, First Grade
Marianne Strayton, First Grade
Hae Jung Yang, First Grade

Wendy Keehfus-Jones, Second Grade
Susan Midlarsky, Second Grade
Jenny Petrosino, Second Grade
Colleen Sheeron, Second Grade
Nancy Sommer, Second Grade
Lisa Watts-Lawton, Second Grade
MaryJo Wieland, Second Grade
Jessa Woods, Second Grade

Eric Angel, Third Grade
Greg Gorman, Third Grade
Susan Lee, Third Grade
Cristina Metcalf, Third Grade
Ann Rose Santoro, Third Grade
Kevin Tougher, Third Grade
Victoria Peacock, Third Grade
Saffron VanGalder, Third Grade

Katrina Abdussalaam, Fourth Grade
Kelly Alsup, Fourth Grade
Patti Dieck, Fourth Grade
Mary Jones, Fourth Grade
Soojin Lu, Fourth Grade
Tricia Salerno, Fourth Grade
Gail Smith, Fourth Grade
Eric Welch, Fourth Grade
Sam Wertheim, Fourth Grade
Erin Wheeler, Fourth Grade

Leslie Arceneaux, Fifth Grade
Adam Baker, Fifth Grade
Janice Fan, Fifth Grade
Peggy Golden, Fifth Grade
Halle Kananak, Fifth Grade
Shauntina Kerrison, Fifth Grade
Pat Mohr, Fifth Grade
Chris Sarlo, Fifth Grade

Additional Writers

Bill Davidson, Fluency Specialist
Robin Hecht, UDL Specialist
Simon Pfeil, Mathematician

Document Management Team

Tam Le, Document Manager
Jennifer Merchan, Copy Editor

Table of Contents

GRADE 2 • MODULE 5

Addition and Subtraction Within 1,000 with Word Problems to 100

Grade 2 • Module 5

Addition and Subtraction Within 1,000 with Word Problems to 100

OVERVIEW

In Module 4, students developed addition and subtraction fluency within 100 and began developing conceptual understanding of the standard algorithm via place value strategies. In Module 5, students build upon their mastery of renaming place value units and extend their work with conceptual understanding of the addition and subtraction algorithms to numbers within 1,000, always with the option of modeling with materials or drawings. Throughout the module, students continue to focus on strengthening and deepening conceptual understanding and fluency.

Topic A focuses on place value strategies to add and subtract within 1,000 (**2.NBT.7**). Students relate *100 more* and *100 less* to addition and subtraction of 100 (**2.NBT.8**). They add and subtract multiples of 100, including counting on to subtract (e.g., for 650 – 300, they start at 300 and think, "300 more gets me to 600, and 50 more gets me to 650, so... 350"). Students also use simplifying strategies for addition and subtraction: they extend the *make a ten* strategy to make a hundred, mentally decomposing one addend to make a hundred with the other (e.g., 299 + 6 becomes 299 + 1 + 5, or 300 + 5, which equals 305) and use compensation to subtract from three-digit numbers (e.g., for 376 – 59, add 1 to each, 377 – 60 = 317). The topic ends with students sharing and critiquing solution strategies for addition and subtraction problems. Throughout the topic, students use place value language and properties of operations to explain why their strategies work (**2.NBT.9**).

In Topics B and C, students continue to build on Module 4's work, now composing and decomposing tens and hundreds within 1,000 (**2.NBT.7**). As each of these topics begins, students relate manipulative representations to the algorithm, then transition to making math drawings in place of the manipulatives. As always, students use place value reasoning and properties of operations to explain their work.

Throughout Module 5, students maintain addition and subtraction fluency within 100 as they use these skills during their daily application work to solve one- and two-step word problems of all types (**2.NBT.5, 2.OA.1**). The focus of concept development is reserved for adding and subtracting within 1,000; using concrete models or drawings and strategies based on place value, properties of operations, and/or the relationship between addition and subtraction; and relating strategies to a written method (**2.NBT.7**). Note that a written method can include number bonds, chip models, arrow notation, the algorithm, or tape diagrams. Many students will need to record these strategies in order to solve correctly. The lessons are designed to provide ample time for discussions that center on student reasoning, explaining why their addition and subtraction strategies work (**2.NBT.9**). For example, students may use the relationship between addition and subtraction to demonstrate why their subtraction solution is correct.

The module culminates with Topic D, wherein students synthesize their understanding of addition and subtraction strategies and choose which strategy is most efficient for given problems. They defend their choices using place value language and their understanding of the properties of operations (**2.NBT.9**).

The Mid-Module Assessment follows Topic B. The End-of-Module Assessment follows Topic D.

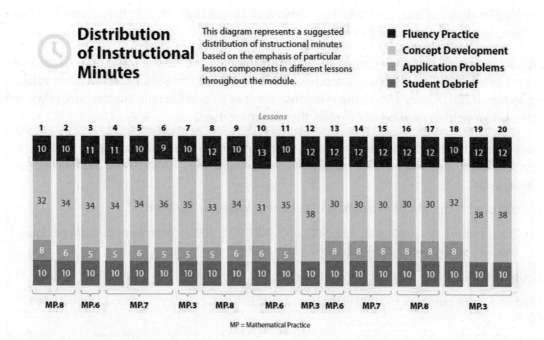

Focus Grade Level Standards

Use place value understanding and properties of operations to add and subtract.

2.NBT.7   Add and subtract within 1000, using concrete models or drawings and strategies based on place value, properties of operations, and/or the relationship between addition and subtraction; relate the strategy to a written method. Understand that in adding or subtracting three-digit numbers, one adds or subtracts hundreds and hundreds, tens and tens, ones and ones; and sometimes it is necessary to compose or decompose tens or hundreds.

2.NBT.8   Mentally add 10 or 100 to a given number 100–900, and mentally subtract 10 or 100 from a given number 100–900.

2.NBT.9   Explain why addition and subtraction strategies work, using place value and the properties of operations. (Explanations may be supported by drawings or objects.)

Foundational Standards

1.OA.3   Apply properties of operations as strategies to add and subtract. *Examples: If 8 + 3 = 11 is known, then 3 + 8 = 11 is also known. (Commutative property of addition.) To add 2 + 6 + 4, the second two numbers can be added to make a ten, so 2 + 6 + 4 = 2 + 10 = 12. (Associative property of addition.)*

Module 5:   Addition and Subtraction Within 1,000 with Word Problems to 100
Date: 10/23/13

iii

1.OA.4   Understand subtraction as an unknown-addend problem. *For example, subtract 10 − 8 by finding the number that makes 10 when added to 8.*

1.NBT.5   Given a two-digit number, mentally find 10 more or 10 less than the number, without having to count; explain the reasoning used.

1.NBT.6   Subtract multiples of 10 in the range 10–90 from multiples of 10 in the range 10–90 (positive or zero differences), using concrete models or drawings and strategies based on place value, properties of operations, and/or the relationship between addition and subtraction; relate the strategy to a written method and explain the reasoning used.

2.NBT.1   Understand that the three digits of a three-digit number represent amounts of hundreds, tens, and ones; e.g., 706 equals 7 hundreds, 0 tens, and 6 ones. Understand the following as special cases:

     a.   100 can be thought of as a bundle of ten tens—called a "hundred."

     b.   The numbers 100, 200, 300, 400, 500, 600, 700, 800, 900 refer to one, two, three, four, five, six, seven, eight, or nine hundreds (and 0 tens and 0 ones).

2.NBT.2   Count within 1000; skip-count by 5s, 10s, and 100s.

2.NBT.3   Read and write numbers to 1000 using base-ten numerals, number names, and expanded form.

2.NBT.5   Fluently add and subtract within 100 using strategies based on place value, properties of operations, and/or the relationship between addition and subtraction.

Focus Standards for Mathematical Practice

MP.3   **Construct viable arguments and critique the reasoning of others.** Students use place value reasoning to explain how each step in their drawing relates to a step in the written method. They choose and explain various solution strategies such as number bonds, chip models, the vertical method, arrow notation, and tape diagrams. They critique the reasoning of others when they listen to their peers explain their strategies for solving problems, and they discuss the efficacy of those strategies.

MP.6   **Attend to precision.** Students attend to precision when they use place value language to explain their math drawings and calculations. They articulate the arithmetic properties they use to solve a variety of problems. For example, when adding 825 + 80, a student may show understanding of the associative property by saying, "I know that 20 + 80 equals 100, so I added 800 + 100 + 5, which equals 905."

MP.7   **Look for and make use of structure.** Students look for and make use of the base ten structure when composing and decomposing. They extend their understanding from Module 4, viewing 10 tens as forming a new unit called a *hundred,* just as they understand that 10 ones forms 1 ten. They apply this understanding of base ten structure when adding and subtracting three-digit numbers, repeatedly bundling and unbundling groups of ten. They also make use of structure when they use simplifying strategies, such as compensation, to create a multiple of ten or a hundred.

	Module 5:	Addition and Subtraction Within 1,000 with Word Problems to 100	
	Date:	10/23/13	**iv**

MP.8 **Look for and express regularity in repeated reasoning.** As students repeatedly manipulate models and record the work abstractly, they recognize the cyclic pattern of the addition or subtraction of like units and the subsequent potential composition or decomposition of units through the place values. They see that the written form represents the same cycle they use with the manipulatives.

Overview of Module Topics and Lesson Objectives

Standards		Topics and Objectives	Days
2.NBT.7 **2.NBT.8** **2.NBT.9**	A	**Strategies for Adding and Subtracting Within 1,000**	7
		Lesson 1: Relate 10 more, 10 less, 100 more, and 100 less to addition and subtraction of 10 and 100.	
		Lesson 2: Add and subtract multiples of 100 including counting on to subtract.	
		Lesson 3: Add multiples of 100 and some tens within 1,000.	
		Lesson 4: Subtract multiples of 100 and some tens within 1,000.	
		Lesson 5: Use the associative property to make a hundred in one addend.	
		Lesson 6: Use the associative property to subtract from three-digit numbers and verify solutions with addition.	
		Lesson 7: Share and critique solution strategies for varied addition and subtraction problems within 1,000.	
2.NBT.7 **2.NBT.9**	B	**Strategies for Composing Tens and Hundreds Within 1,000**	5
		Lessons 8–9: Relate manipulative representations to the addition algorithm.	
		Lessons 10–11: Use math drawings to represent additions with up to two compositions and relate drawings to the addition algorithm.	
		Lesson 12: Choose and explain solution strategies and record with a written addition method.	
		Mid-Module Assessment: Topics A–B (assessment 1/2 day, return 1/2 day, remediation or further applications 1 day)	2
2.NBT.7 **2.NBT.9**	C	**Strategies for Decomposing Tens and Hundreds Within 1,000**	6
		Lesson 13: Relate manipulative representations to the subtraction algorithm, and use addition to explain why the subtraction method works.	
		Lessons 14–15: Use math drawings to represent subtraction with up to two decompositions, relate drawings to the algorithm, and use addition to explain why the subtraction method works.	

Module 5:   Addition and Subtraction Within 1,000 with Word Problems to 100
Date: 10/23/13

v

Standards		Topics and Objectives	Days
		Lessons 16–17: Subtract from multiples of 100 and from numbers with zero in the tens place.	
		Lesson 18: Apply and explain alternate methods for subtracting from multiples of 100 and from numbers with zero in the tens place.	
2.NBT.7 2.NBT.8 2.NBT.9	D	**Student Explanations for Choice of Solution Methods** Lessons 19–20: Choose and explain solution strategies and record with a written addition or subtraction method.	2
		End-of-Module Assessment: Topics A–D (assessment 1/2 day, return 1/2 day, remediation or further applications 1 day)	2
Total Number of Instructional Days			**24**

Terminology

New or Recently Introduced Terms

- Algorithm (a step-by-step procedure to solve a particular type of problem)
- Compensation (simplifying strategy where students add or subtract the same amount to or from both numbers to create an equivalent but easier problem)
- Compose (e.g., to make 1 larger unit from 10 smaller units)
- Decompose (e.g., to break 1 larger unit into 10 smaller units)
- New groups below (show newly composed units on the line below the appropriate place in the addition algorithm)
- Simplifying strategy (e.g., to solve 299 + 6, think 299 + 1 + 5 = 300 + 5 = 305.)

Familiar Terms and Symbols[1]

- Addend
- Addition
- Bundle
- Difference
- Equation
- Number bond
- Place value
- Place value chart (pictured right)
- Place value or number disk (pictured above right)

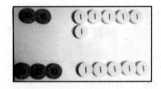

Place value disks

Place Value Chart with Headings
(use with numbers)

hundreds	tens	ones
7	2	6

---

[1] These are terms and symbols students have seen previously.

- Rename
- Subtraction
- Tape diagram
- Total
- Unbundle
- Units of ones, tens, hundreds

Place Value Chart without Headings
(use with number disks)

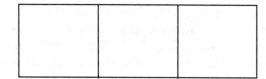

Suggested Tools and Representations

- Arrow notation, arrow way
- Chip model (pictured right)
- Number bond
- Place value charts and mats (pictured above right)
- Place value disk sets (18 ones, 18 tens, 18 hundreds, 1 one thousand per set)
- Tape diagram

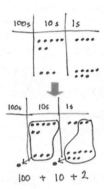

Chip model

Note: Students work through a progression of models to represent the addition and subtraction algorithm. Following the use of actual place value disks, students learn to draw the disks to represent numbers. This model provides an added level of support in that students write the value on each disk (see image below left). Because the value is on the disk, there is no need to label the place value chart. Next, students learn the chip model, drawing dots on a labeled place value chart (see image below right). While still pictorial, this model is more abstract because the value of the chip derives from its placement on the chart.

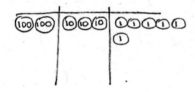

Place value disk drawing

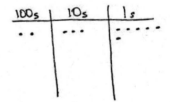

Chip model

Scaffolds[2]

The scaffolds integrated into *A Story of Units* give alternatives for how students access information as well as express and demonstrate their learning. Strategically placed margin notes are provided within each lesson elaborating on the use of specific scaffolds at applicable times. They address many needs presented by English language learners, students with disabilities, students performing above grade level, and students performing below grade level. Many of the suggestions are organized by Universal Design for Learning (UDL) principles and are applicable to more than one population. To read more about the approach to differentiated instruction in *A Story of Units,* please refer to "How to Implement *A Story of Units.*"

Assessment Summary

Type	Administered	Format	Standards Addressed
Mid-Module Assessment Task	After Topic B	Constructed response with rubric	2.NBT.7 2.NBT.8 2.NBT.9
End-of-Module Assessment Task	After Topic D	Constructed response with rubric	2.NBT.7 2.NBT.8 2.NBT.9

[2] Students with disabilities may require Braille, large print, audio, or special digital files. Please visit the website, www.p12.nysed.gov/specialed/aim, for specific information on how to obtain student materials that satisfy the National Instructional Materials Accessibility Standard (NIMAS) format.

Topic A

Strategies for Adding and Subtracting Within 1,000

2.NBT.7, 2.NBT.8, 2.NBT.9

Focus Standards:	2.NBT.7	Add and subtract within 1000, using concrete models or drawings and strategies based on place value, properties of operations, and/or the relationship between addition and subtraction; relate the strategy to a written method. Understand that in adding or subtracting three-digit numbers, one adds or subtracts hundreds and hundreds, tens and tens, ones and ones; and sometimes it is necessary to compose or decompose tens or hundreds.
	2.NBT.8	Mentally add 10 or 100 to a given number 100–900, and mentally subtract 10 or 100 from a given number 100–900.
	2.NBT.9	Explain why addition and subtraction strategies work, using place value and the properties of operations. (Explanations may be supported by drawings or objects.)
Instructional Days:	7	
Coherence -Links from:	G1–M6	Place Value, Comparison, Addition and Subtraction to 100
-Links to:	G3–M2	Place Value and Problem Solving with Units of Measure

In Topic A, students practice the simplifying strategies they learned in Module 4, but with numbers up to 1,000. They will be asked to consider which strategy is most efficient for each problem they encounter.

In Lesson 1, students relate *100 more, 100 less, 10 more, and 10 less* to addition and subtraction. They recognize that they must still add and subtract like units, and that the digit in the hundreds place changes when adding and subtracting 100, just as the digit in the tens place changes when adding or subtracting 10. Students see numbers in terms of place value units: 290 – 100 is 2 hundreds 9 tens minus 1 hundred. They learn to record the addition and subtraction of multiples of 100 using arrow notation (i.e., the arrow way).

$$320 + 200$$

$$320 \xrightarrow{+100} 420 \xrightarrow{+100} 520$$

In Lesson 2, students add and subtract multiples of 100 by counting on by hundreds. For example, when adding 200 to 320, they may count up from 320: 420, 520. Students also develop flexibility in using related addition problems. For example, to solve 519 – 200, one student might think "5 hundreds minus 2 hundreds is 3 hundreds, plus 19 is 319," while another starts at 200, adds on 19 and then 3 hundreds to reach 519, so 319.

In Lessons 3 and 4, students continue to add and subtract multiples of 100 with the added complexity of some tens. Problems are chosen so that at first the tens digit is close to a multiple of 100 (e.g., 190, 290, 380) to make it easier to form the next hundred by decomposing addends. This prompts students to analyze and use relationships between numbers to develop a variety of simplifying strategies.

Students also use arrow notation to record their mental math. First, they add a multiple of 100, and then count on by multiples of 10 to find the total (as shown at right). Lesson 3 focuses on addition, while Lesson 4 emphasizes related strategies for subtraction.

$$320 + 270$$
$$320 \xrightarrow{+200} 520 \xrightarrow{+70} 590$$

In Lesson 5, students apply the use of number bonds to decompose larger numbers, just as they did with numbers within 100. For example, when solving 320 + 290, they can break 320 into 10 and 310 to make 310 + 300 = 610 (as shown at right), just as they would have decomposed to add 32 and 29 in Module 4. They realize the problem can be conceived of as 32 tens + 29 tens. Note that arrow notation can also be used to solve 320 + 290 by first adding 200, then 80, and then 10, or by adding 300 and then subtracting 10. Students also work with problems such as 298 + 137, using a number bond to decompose 137 into 2 and 135, thus creating the equivalent but easier equation 300 + 135 = 435.

$$320 + 290 = 310 + 300$$
$$\overset{\wedge}{310} \; 10$$
$$= 610$$

I can decompose 320 as 10 and 310 to make 300 and 310.

In Lesson 6, the ease of subtracting a multiple of 100 is highlighted again, as students extend their work from Module 4 using compensation (i.e., the associative property) for subtraction. Students may add or subtract a multiple of 10 to make an equivalent problem that involves no renaming. For example, when subtracting 610 – 290, the same number, 10, can be added to both numbers to create a multiple of 100 (as shown at right). Students also solve problems such as 451 – 195, adding 5 to both the minuend and subtrahend to make 456 – 200.

$$610 - 290 = 620 - 300$$
$$= 320$$

If I add the same amount to both numbers, the difference stays the same!

Topic A closes with Lesson 7, which provides students the opportunity to solidify their new skills. They confront a variety of problems, solve them, and then share their solution strategies. Through spirited discussion, students critique the work of their peers while deepening their understanding of various strategies.

The strategies taught in Topic A are designed to develop students' conceptual understanding of addition and subtraction using models, drawings, properties of operations, and strategies based on place value. At the same time, students relate these strategies to written methods such as arrow notation and number bonds. This sets the stage for flexible thinking as students move into composing and decomposing units in Topics B and C.

A Teaching Sequence Towards Mastery of Strategies for Adding and Subtracting Within 1,000

Objective 1: Relate 10 more, 10 less, 100 more, and 100 less to addition and subtraction of 10 and 100.
(Lesson 1)

Objective 2: Add and subtract multiples of 100 including counting on to subtract.
(Lesson 2)

Objective 3: Add multiples of 100 and some tens within 1,000.
(Lesson 3)

Objective 4: Subtract multiples of 100 and some tens within 1,000.
(Lesson 4)

Objective 5: Use the associative property to make a hundred in one addend.
(Lesson 5)

Objective 6: Use the associative property to subtract from three-digit numbers and verify solutions with addition.
(Lesson 6)

Objective 7: Share and critique solution strategies for varied addition and subtraction problems within 1,000.
(Lesson 7)

Lesson 1

Objective: Relate 10 more, 10 less, 100 more, and 100 less to addition and subtraction of 10 and 100.

Suggested Lesson Structure

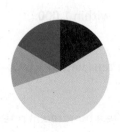

■ Fluency Practice   (10 minutes)
■ Application Problem   (8 minutes)
■ Concept Development   (32 minutes)
■ Student Debrief   (10 minutes)
  Total Time   **(60 minutes)**

Fluency Practice (10 minutes)

- Place Value **2.NBT.1, 2.NBT.5**   (6 minutes)
- More/Less **2.NBT.5**   (4 minutes)

Place Value (6 minutes)

Materials: (T) Place value chart (S) Personal white boards, place value charts

Note: Practicing place value skills will prepare students for adding and subtracting 10 and 100 in the lesson.

- T: (Project place value chart to the hundreds.) Show 6 ones in chips. Write the number below it.
- S: (Draw 6 chips in the ones column and write 6 below it.)
- T: Show 1 chip in the tens column and write the number below it.
- S: (Draw 1 chip in the tens column and write 1 at the bottom of the tens column.)
- T: Say the number the Say Ten way.
- S: 1 ten 6.
- T: Say the number in standard form.
- S: 16.
- T: Add 1 chip to your tens column. What is 10 more than 16?
- S: 26.
- T: The Say Ten way?
- S: 2 tens 6.
- T: Now add 1 chip to your hundreds column. What is 100 more than 26?
- S: 126.

Lesson 1:   Relate 10 more, 10 less, 100 more, and 100 less to addition and
          subtraction of 10 and 100.   5.A.4
Date: 10/23/13

T: The Say Ten way?

S: 1 hundred 2 tens 6.

T: Cross out a chip in the tens column. What is 10 less than 126?

S: 116.

T: The Say Ten way?

S: 1 hundred 1 ten 6.

T: Cross out a chip in the hundreds column. What is 100 less than 116?

S: 16.

Continue with the following possible sequence: 254, 310, 505.

More/Less (4 minutes)

Note: Practicing giving 10 or 100 more or less will prepare students to add and subtract 10 and 100 fluently.

T: For every number I say, you say a number that is 10 more. When I say 5, you say 15. Ready?

T: 10.

S: 20.

T: 5.

S: 15.

Continue with the following possible sequence: 19, 67, 90, 95, 110, 111, 139, 156, 256, 299, 305, 319.

T: Now for every number I say, you say a number that is 10 less. When I say 20, you say 10. Ready?

T: 20.

S: 10.

T: 22.

S: 12.

Continue with the following possible sequence: 19, 78, 100, 107, 182, 201, 299, 312, 321.

T: Let's try saying 100 more for every number I say. When I say 56, you say 156. Ready?

T: 56.

S: 156.

T: 37.

S: 137.

Continue with the following possible sequence: 80, 8, 88, 288, 300, 333, 566, 900.

T: Now for every number I say, you say a number that is 100 less. When I say 150, you say 50. Ready?

T: 150.

S: 50.

T: 159.

S: 59.

Lesson 1:   Relate 10 more, 10 less, 100 more, and 100 less to addition and
              subtraction of 10 and 100.
Date: 10/23/13

5.A.5

Continue with the following possible sequence: 168, 170, 270, 277, 400, 404, 434.

Application Problem (8 minutes)

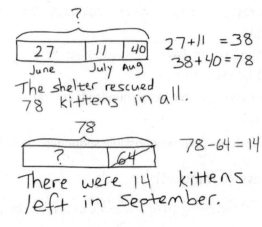

27+11 =38
38+40=78
The shelter rescued 78 kittens in all.

78-64 =14
There were 14 kittens left in September.

The shelter rescued 27 kittens in June. In July, it rescued 11 more. In August, it rescued 40 more.

How many kittens did the shelter rescue during those 3 months?

If 64 of those kittens found homes by August, how many still needed homes?

Note: This problem is designed to lead into the Concept Development for the day's lesson, relating 10 more and 10 less to addition and subtraction. Students will complete this problem independently to provide insight into the kinds of mental strategies they currently use.

Review the RDW procedure for problem solving: Read the problem, draw and label, write a number sentence, and write a word sentence. The more students participate in reasoning through problems with a systematic approach, the more they internalize those behaviors and thought processes.

(Excerpted from "How to Implement *A Story of Units*.")

Concept Development (32 minutes)

Materials: (T) Set of sentence frames as shown to the
            right (S) 7 hundreds disks, 9 tens disks, 9
            ones disks, place value charts

Post *more* sentence frames on one side of the board and *less* frames on the other side. Pass out charts and disks.

10 more than ___ is ___. ___ is 10 more than ___.	10 less than ___ is ___. ___ is 10 less than ___.
100 more than ___ is ___. ___ is 100 more than ___.	100 less than ___ is ___. ___ is 100 less than ___.

MP.8

T: Use your number disks to show me 157 on your place value chart.

S: (Show 1 hundred 5 tens 7 ones.)

T: Show me 10 more.

S: (Add a tens disk to show 1 hundred 6 tens 7 ones.)

T: Use a sentence frame to describe adding 10 to 157.

S: 10 more than 157 is 167. → 167 is 10 more than 157.

T: What did you do to change 157?

S: We added 10 to the tens place. → We added 1 ten to 5 tens.

T: Give me an addition sentence starting with 157.

S: 157 + 10 = 167.

NOTES ON MULTIPLE MEANS OF REPRESENTATION:

Use different models to demonstrate the change in 10 more, 10 less, 100 more, 100 less.

- Use Hide Zero cards to show the changes in place value.

- Use concrete objects other than disks, such as bundled straws or base ten blocks, to show new groups of hundreds and/or tens.

	Lesson 1:	Relate 10 more, 10 less, 100 more, and 100 less to addition and subtraction of 10 and 100.
	Date:	10/23/13

5.A.6

T:	Start with 167.
S:	167 = 10 + 157. → 167 = 157 + 10.

(Repeat the process for 10 less than 157.)

T:	Show me 157 again. (Pause as students reset their place value charts.)
T:	Show me 100 more than 157.
S:	(Add a hundreds disk to show 2 hundreds 5 tens 7 ones.)
T:	Use a sentence frame to describe adding 100 to 157.
S:	257 is 100 more than 157. → 100 more than 157 is 257.
T:	What did you do to change 157?
S:	We added another hundred. → We added 1 hundred to 1 hundred.
T:	Be specific. Where did you add the hundred?
S:	To the hundreds place.
T:	Yes!
T:	Give me an addition sentence starting with 157.
S:	157 + 100 = 257.
T:	Start with 257.
S:	257 = 100 + 157. → 257 = 157 + 100.

MP.8

NOTES ON MULTIPLE MEANS OF ACTION AND EXPRESSION:

Listen intently as students use place value language to talk with their partners. Use number disks and place value charts to help students navigate the following vocabulary: *place value, hundreds, tens, ones, digit, value,* and *unit*. Add new vocabulary to the wall and point to words accompanied by a visual.

Repeat the process for 100 less than 157.

T:	Talk with your partner. Use place value language to explain what you understand about 10 more, 10 less, 100 more, and 100 less. (Allow about one minute for discussion.)
S:	We already knew about 10 more and 10 less, and now 100 acts the same. → 10 less and 100 less is the same as taking away 10 or 100. → We have to subtract and add the same units, so the tens place changes when we add or subtract 10. The same for the hundreds place.
T:	(Collect the number disks and charts.) Listen as I say a number pattern. Raise your hand when you know the *more* or *less* rule for my pattern.
T:	For example, if I say, "121, 131, 141, 151, 161," you say, "10 more." Wait for my signal. Ready?
T:	135, 145, 155, 165, 175.
S:	10 more!
T:	282, 272, 262, 252, 242.
S:	10 less!

Continue until students can readily identify the rule.

T:	Take out your personal boards. Now I'll write a series of numbers on the board. You write the rule and the next three numbers. The rules are + 10, − 10, + 100, and − 100.
T:	Turn your board over when you have written your answer. Wait until I say, "Show me." Ready?

Lesson 1:

Date:

Relate 10 more, 10 less, 100 more, and 100 less to addition and subtraction of 10 and 100.

10/23/13

5.A.7

T: (Write 67, 57, 47, ___, ___, ___. Pause.) Show me.

S: (Show – 10 and 37, 27, 17.)

Continue to give students practice with each rule.

In this next activity, model arrow notation by recording the following sequence on the board step by step as students write each answer.

It will look like this: 542 $\xrightarrow{+100}$ ___ $\xrightarrow{-10}$ ___ $\xrightarrow{-10}$ ___ $\xrightarrow{-100}$ ___ $\xrightarrow{-100}$ ___.

T: Let's try something different. (Write 542 $\xrightarrow{+100}$ ___ on the board.) What is 542 + 100? Show me.

S: (Write 642.)

T: – 10? (Continue to record the sequence by filling in 642 and writing $\xrightarrow{-10}$ ___.)

S: (Write 632.)

T: – 10? (Fill in 632 and write $\xrightarrow{-10}$ ___.)

S: (Write 622.)

T: – 100? (Fill in 622 and write $\xrightarrow{-100}$ ___.)

S: (Write 522.)

T: – 100? (Fill in 522 and write $\xrightarrow{-100}$ ___.)

S: (Write 422.)

$$542 \xrightarrow{+100} 642 \xrightarrow{-10} 632 \xrightarrow{-10} 622 \xrightarrow{-100} 522 \xrightarrow{-100} 422$$

T: (Point to the completed sequence on the board.) In the last module, we used this simplifying strategy; we called it the arrow way. Talk to your partner about how this example is the same as and different from the ones we've done before.

S: Instead of ones and tens, this is tens and hundreds. → It's just different place values. Everything else is the same. → It shows that you're changing the ones or the tens place and whether it's more or less.

If necessary or if time permits, model another example with the following problem:

367 – 220.

224 $\xrightarrow{-100}$ ___ $\xrightarrow{-100}$ ___ $\xrightarrow{-10}$ ___ $\xrightarrow{-10}$ ___.

Problem Set (10 minutes)

Students should do their personal best to complete the Problem Set within the allotted 10 minutes. Some problems do not specify a method for solving. This is an intentional reduction of scaffolding that invokes MP.5, Use Appropriate Tools Strategically. Students should solve these problems using the RDW approach used for Application Problems.

For some classes, it may be appropriate to modify the assignment by specifying which problems students should work on first. With this option, let the careful sequencing of the problem set guide your selections so that problems continue to be scaffolded. Balance word problems with other problem types to ensure a range

Lesson 1:   Relate 10 more, 10 less, 100 more, and 100 less to addition and
Date: subtraction of 10 and 100.
              10/23/13

5.A.8

of practice. Assign incomplete problems for homework or at another time during the day.

Student Debrief (10 minutes)

Lesson Objective: Relate 10 more, 10 less, 100 more, and 100 less to addition and subtraction of 10 and 100.

The Student Debrief is intended to invite reflection and active processing of the total lesson experience.

Invite students to review their solutions for the Problem Set. They should check work by comparing answers with a partner before going over answers as a class. Look for misconceptions or misunderstandings that can be addressed in the Debrief. Guide students in a conversation to debrief the Problem Set and process the lesson.

You may choose to use any combination of the questions below to lead the discussion.

- What makes Problems 1(e) and (f) more challenging? In Problem 1(e), does *10 more* mean we should add 10 to 319? Why not? In Problem 1(f), why did you add 100 to 499 when it says *100 less*?

- What do you need to know to complete each pattern in Problem 2?

- In Problem 3(b), what total quantity did you subtract from 187? How can you write it as an equation?

- In Problem 4(b), what total quantity did you add to 323 to arrive at 400? How did you show the missing addend using the arrow way? How can we show it as an equation?

- Which simplifying strategy did we use today to record a sequence of numbers? How is it helpful?

- What important connection did we make today? What are we actually doing when we talk about 10 more, 10 less, 100 more, 100 less than a number?

Name Chris   Date

1. Complete each *more* or *less* statement.
   a. 10 more than 175 is __185__.   b. 100 more than 175 is __275__.
   c. 10 less than 175 is __165__.   d. 100 less than 175 is __75__.
   e. 319 is 10 more than __309__.   f. 499 is 100 less than __599__.
   g. __788__ is 100 less than 888.   h. __503__ is 10 more than 493.
   i. 898 is __100 less__ than 998.   j. 607 is __10 more__ than 597.
   k. 10 more than 309 is __319__.   l. 309 is __10 less__ than 319.

2. Complete each regular number pattern.
   a. 170, 180, 190, __200__, __210__, __220__
   b. 420, 410, 400, __390__, __380__, __370__
   c. 789, 689, __589__, __489__, __389__ 289
   d. 565, 575, __585__, __595__, __605__ 615
   e. 724, __714__, __704__, __694__, 684, 674
   f. __916__, __906__, __896__, 886, 876, 866

3. Complete each statement.

   a. 389 $\xrightarrow{+10}$ __399__ $\xrightarrow{+100}$ 499   b. 187 $\xrightarrow{-100}$ __87__ $\xrightarrow{-10}$ __77__

   c. 609 $\xrightarrow{-10}$ __599__ $\xrightarrow{-100}$ 499 $\xrightarrow{+10}$ __509__ $\xrightarrow{+10}$ 519

   d. 512 $\xrightarrow{-10}$ __502__ $\xrightarrow{-10}$ __492__ $\xrightarrow{+100}$ __592__ $\xrightarrow{+100}$ __692__ $\xrightarrow{+10}$ __702__.

4. Solve using the arrow way.

   a. 212 + 106 = __212__ $\xrightarrow{+100}$ 312 $\xrightarrow{+6}$ 318

   323 $\xrightarrow{+10}$ 393 $\xrightarrow{+7}$ 400

   b. 323 + __77__ = 400

   c. __221__ + 511 = 732   511 $\xrightarrow{+200}$ 711 $\xrightarrow{+20}$ 731 $\xrightarrow{+1}$ 732

COMMON CORE

Lesson 1:   Relate 10 more, 10 less, 100 more, and 100 less to addition and
              subtraction of 10 and 100.
Date: 10/23/13

5.A.9

Exit Ticket (3 minutes)

After the Student Debrief, instruct students to complete the Exit Ticket. A review of their work will help you assess the students' understanding of the concepts that were presented in the lesson today and plan more effectively for future lessons. You may read the questions aloud to the students.

Lesson 1:   Relate 10 more, 10 less, 100 more, and 100 less to addition and
              subtraction of 10 and 100.
Date: 10/23/13

5.A.10

Name _____   Date _____

1. Complete each *more* or *less* statement.

   a. 10 more than 175 is _____.

   b. 100 more than 175 is _____.

   c. 10 less than 175 is _____.

   d. 100 less than 175 is _____.

   e. 319 is 10 more than _____.

   f. 499 is 100 less than _____.

   g. _____ is 100 less than 888.

   h. _____ is 10 more than 493.

   i. 898 is _____ than 998.

   j. 607 is _____ than 597.

   k. 10 more than 309 is _____.

   l. 309 is _____ than 319.

2. Complete each regular number pattern.

   a. 170, 180, 190, _____, _____, _____

   b. 420, 410, 400, _____, _____, _____

   c. 789, 689, _____, _____, _____, 289

   d. 565, 575, _____, _____, _____, 615

   e. 724, _____, _____, _____, 684, 674

   f. _____, _____, _____, 886, 876, 866

COMMON CORE™

Lesson 1:   Relate 10 more, 10 less, 100 more, and 100 less to addition and
            subtraction of 10 and 100.
Date: 10/23/13

5.A.11

3. Complete each statement.

a. 389 $\xrightarrow{+10}$ ____ $\xrightarrow{+100}$ ____

b. 187 $\xrightarrow{-100}$ ____ $\xrightarrow{-10}$ ____

c. 609 $\xrightarrow{-10}$ ____ $\xrightarrow{\ \underline{\quad}\ }$ 499 $\xrightarrow{+10}$ ____ $\xrightarrow{+\ \underline{\quad}}$ 519

d. 512 $\xrightarrow{-10}$ ____ $\xrightarrow{-10}$ ____ $\xrightarrow{+100}$ ____ $\xrightarrow{+100}$ ____ $\xrightarrow{+10}$ ____

4. Solve using the arrow way.

a. 212 + 106 = _____

b. 323 + _____ = 400

c. _____ + 511 = 732

Lesson 1:   Relate 10 more, 10 less, 100 more, and 100 less to addition and
subtraction of 10 and 100.
Date: 10/23/13

5.A.12

Name _____ Date _____

Solve using the arrow way.

1. 448 + 206 = _____

2. 679 + _____ = 890

3. _____ + 765 = 945

COMMON CORE™

Lesson 1: Relate 10 more, 10 less, 100 more, and 100 less to addition and subtraction of 10 and 100.

Date: 10/23/13

5.A.13

Name _____   Date _____

1. Complete each *more* or *less* statement.

   a. 10 more than 222 is _____.   b. 100 more than 222 is _____.

   c. 10 less than 222 is _____.   d. 100 less than 222 is _____.

   e. 515 is 10 more than _____.   f. 299 is 100 less than _____.

   g. _____ is 100 less than 345.   h. _____ is 10 more than 397.

   i. 898 is _____ than 998.   j. 607 is _____ than 597.

   k. 10 more than 309 is _____.   l. 309 is _____ than 319.

2. Complete each regular number pattern.

   a. 280, 290, _____, _____, _____, 330

   b. 530, 520, 510, _____, _____, _____

   c. 643, 543, _____, _____, _____, 143

   d. 681, 691, _____, _____, _____, 731

   e. 427, _____, _____, _____, 387, 377

   f. _____, _____, _____, 788, 778, 768

COMMON CORE™

Lesson 1: Relate 10 more, 10 less, 100 more, and 100 less to addition and
           subtraction of 10 and 100.
Date: 10/23/13

5.A.14

3. Complete each statement.

   a. 235 $\xrightarrow{+10}$ ____ $\xrightarrow{+100}$ ____

   b. 391 $\xrightarrow{-100}$ _____ $\xrightarrow{-10}$ _____

   c. 417 $\xrightarrow{-10}$ _____ $\xrightarrow{-\_\_\_}$ _____ $\xrightarrow{-100}$ 297

   d. 311 $\xrightarrow{-10}$ _____ $\xrightarrow{-10}$ _____ $\xrightarrow{+100}$ _____ $\xrightarrow{+100}$ _____ $\xrightarrow{+10}$ _____

4. Solve using the arrow way.

   a. 376 + 103 = _____

   b. 290 + _____ = 400

   c. _____ + 712 = 852

Lesson 2

Objective: Add and subtract multiples of 100 including counting on to subtract.

Suggested Lesson Structure

▨ Application Problem	(6 minutes)	
■ Fluency Practice	(10 minutes)	
▨ Concept Development	(34 minutes)	
■ Student Debrief	(10 minutes)	
Total Time	**(60 minutes)**	

Application Problem (6 minutes)

Max has 42 marbles in his marble bag after he added 20 marbles at noon. How many marbles did he have before noon?

Note: This problem gives students a chance to apply their new learning and to practice an *add to with start unknown* problem, as in G2–Module 4. Many students will say 62 marbles. Encourage them to represent the problem using a number bond if they are struggling. This way, they will see the part–whole relationship modeled differently.

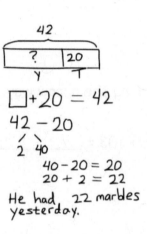

Fluency Practice (10 minutes)

- Place Value **2.NBT.1, 2.NBT.7**   (7 minutes)
- How Many More Hundreds? **2.NBT.7**   (3 minutes)

Place Value (7 minutes)

Materials: (T) Place value chart (S) Personal white boards, place value charts

Note: Practicing place value skills prepares students for adding and subtracting multiples of 100 in the lesson.

- T: (Project place value chart to the hundreds.) Show 1 hundred, 5 tens, and 2 ones in chips on a place value chart. Write the number below it.
- S: (Draw 1 hundred, 5 tens, and 2 ones in chips on a place value chart.)
- T: Say the number in unit form.
- S: 1 hundred 5 tens 2 ones.

Lesson 2:   Add and subtract multiples of 100 including counting on to subtract.
Date: 10/23/13

5.A.16

T: Say the number in unit form using only tens and ones.

S: 15 tens 2 ones.

T: Say the number in unit form using only hundreds and ones.

S: 1 hundred 52 ones.

T: Say the number in standard form.

S: 152.

T: Add 2 hundreds to your chart. How many hundreds do you have now?

S: 3 hundreds.

T: What is 200 more than 152?

S: 352.

T: Add 3 hundreds to 352. How many hundreds do you have now?

S: 6 hundreds.

T: What is 300 more than 352?

S: 652.

T: Now subtract 4 hundreds from 652. What is 400 less than 652?

S: 252.

Continue with the following possible sequence: + 500, − 100, + 300, − 900.

How Many More Hundreds? (3 minutes)

Note: Practicing subtracting multiples of 100 prepares students for the lesson.

T: If I say 300 − 200, you say 100. To say it in a sentence, you say, "100 more than 200 is 300." Ready?

T: 300 − 200.

S: 100.

T: Say it in a sentence.

S: 100 more than 200 is 300.

Continue with the following possible sequence: 405 − 305, 801 − 601, 650 − 350, 825 − 125, 999 − 299.

Concept Development (34 minutes)

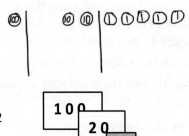

Materials: (T) Hide Zero cards (S) Personal white boards, 9 each of ones, tens, and hundreds disks

Draw a place value chart on the board. Show 125 using Hide Zero cards.

T: Yesterday we added and subtracted 1 hundred. Today, let's add 2 hundreds, then 3 hundreds, and more!

T: How many do you see?

Lesson 2:   Add and subtract multiples of 100 including counting on to subtract.

Date: 10/23/13

S: 125!

T: (Separate the cards.) Say the number in unit form.

S: 1 hundred 2 tens 5 ones.

T: Show me this number with your disks.

S: (Students show 1 hundred, 2 tens, and 5 ones on their charts.)

T: (Draw the disks on the board. Change hundreds card to 300, and put cards together.) How much do you see?

S: 325!

T: How can you show this change using your place value disks?

S: Add 2 more hundreds.

T: Do it.

T: Now I am going to add 2 more hundreds. You do it too. Turn and talk, what will happen to the number when I add 2 hundreds?

S: The number in the hundreds place will get bigger by 2. → The number will get bigger by 200. The ones and tens digits will stay the same. → It will be 525.

T: (Draw 2 more hundreds.) What is 325 + 200?

S: 525!

T: Say it in unit form.

S: 5 hundreds, 2 tens, 5 ones!

T: If I asked you to add 3 hundreds to 450, how could you solve that?

S: Count on by a hundred 3 times. → Change the 4 to 7 because 4 hundreds plus 3 hundreds is 7 hundreds. → Add 3 hundreds disks on the place value chart.

T: Let's show that on the board using both simplifying strategies, the arrow way and number bonds. I know many of you can just do mental math!

T: I can add 3 hundreds using the arrow way, as we did yesterday. (Demonstrate and involve the students as you write.) I can also break apart the hundreds and tens with a number bond, add the hundreds, and then add the tens. (Demonstrate and involve the students as you write.)

T: No matter which way I write it, when I add hundreds to a number, the tens and ones stay the same!

T: Now it's your turn. On your personal board, solve 147 + 200. Show me your board when you have an answer.

Repeat this process with examples as needed: 276 + 300, 382 + 400, and 400 + 516.

NOTES ON MULTIPLE MEANS OF ENGAGEMENT:

During the lesson, encourage a student who struggled with adding tens in G2–Module 4 to explain the process of adding hundreds to the class. This will help the student solidify his understanding and build his confidence. Praise his use of place value language to explain his thinking.

$$450 \xrightarrow{+300} 700$$

$$450 + 300$$
$$400 \quad 50$$
$$400 + 300 = 700$$
$$700 + 50 = 750$$

Lesson 2:   Add and subtract multiples of 100 including counting on to subtract.
Date: 10/23/13

5.A.18

(Show 725 using Hide Zero cards and draw disks on the place value chart on the board.)

T: Now, let's subtract 2 hundreds, then 3 hundreds, and more!

T: How many do you see?

S: 725!

T: Say it in unit form.

S: 7 hundreds 2 tens 5 ones!

T: (Replace the 700 card with 500 and erase 2 hundreds from the chart.) How many do you see?

S: 5 hundreds 2 tens 5 ones.

T: I am going to subtract 2 more hundreds. Turn and talk: What will happen to the number when I subtract 2 hundreds?

S: The number in the hundreds place will get smaller by 2. → The number will get smaller by 200. → It will be 325 because 5 hundreds minus 2 hundreds equals 3 hundreds. The other digits stay the same.

T: (Subtract 2 hundreds.) What is 525 – 200?

S: 325!

T: Say it in unit form.

S: 3 hundreds 2 tens 5 ones!

T: Okay, now let's subtract 3 hundreds from 582. Take a moment and work on your personal board to solve 582 – 300. (Show the work on the board as students work out this first problem using number bonds and the arrow way.)

T: (Model both the number bonds and arrow methods from their work.) We have an extra simplifying strategy when we are subtracting. We can count up from the part we know.

T: What is the whole?

S: 582.

T: What is the part we know?

NOTES ON
MULTIPLE MEANS OF
ACTION AND
EXPRESSION:

Invite a student to be in charge of the place value chart while you work with the Hide Zero cards, or vice versa.

The number bond's decomposition is one choice for solving the problem that may not work for some students as a solution strategy, but is beneficial for all to understand. Students should be encouraged to make connections between different solution strategies and to choose what works best for a given problem or for their way of thinking.

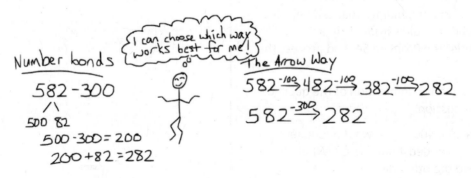

COMMON CORE   Lesson 2:   Add and subtract multiples of 100 including counting on to subtract.

Date: 10/23/13   **5.A.19**

© 2013 Common Core, Inc. All rights reserved. commoncore.org

S: 300.

T: How can we show the missing part with an addition problem?

S: 300 + ___ = 582. → ___ + 300 = 582.

T: We can use the arrow way, counting first by either tens or ones. Try it with a partner.

Guide students through this, or let them work independently. Starting at 300, they might add 2 hundreds first and then 82, or add 82 first and then add 2 hundreds.

Repeat with 620 – 400, 541 – 200, and 797 – 300.

Problem Set (10 minutes)

Students should do their personal best to complete the Problem Set within the allotted 10 minutes. For some classes, it may be appropriate to modify the assignment by specifying which problems they work on first. Some problems do not specify a method for solving. Students solve these problems using the RDW approach used for Application Problems.

Student Debrief (10 minutes)

Lesson Objective: Add and subtract multiples of 100 including counting on to subtract.

The Student Debrief is intended to invite reflection and active processing of the total lesson experience.

Invite students to review their solutions for the Problem Set. They should check work by comparing answers with a partner before going over answers as a class. Look for misconceptions or misunderstandings that can be addressed in the Debrief. Guide students in a conversation to debrief the Problem Set and process the lesson.

You may choose to use any combination of the questions below to lead the discussion.

▪   In Problem 1(c), 400 + 374, what happened to 374 when you added 4 hundreds? What happened to the other digits?

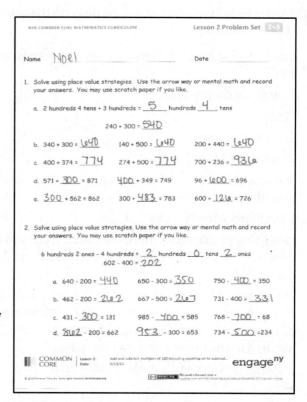

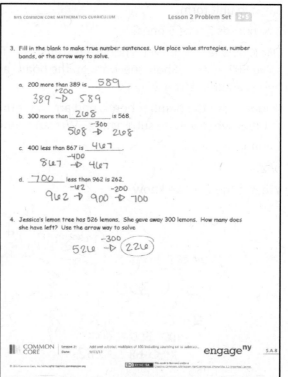

Lesson 2:   Add and subtract multiples of 100 including counting on to subtract.
Date: 10/23/13

5.A.20

- Which strategy did you use to solve the sequence in Problem 1(e)? Why is the arrow way a good choice when you have a missing part, or addend?

- If you were using number disks to show Problem 2(b), 667 – 500, what change would you make on your place value chart? What would stay the same?

- Explain to your partner how you solved the sequence in Problem 2(c). How could you show the missing part with an addition problem? How could you count on from the part you know?

- How was solving Problem 3(a) different from solving Problem 3(b)? Did you add hundreds in both situations? For each problem, did you find the part or whole?

- Explain to your partner which strategies you used to solve Problems 3(c) and (d). Did you use the same strategy for both problems? Can you think of another way to solve these problems?

Exit Ticket (3 minutes)

After the Student Debrief, instruct students to complete the Exit Ticket. A review of their work will help you assess the students' understanding of the concepts that were presented in the lesson today and plan more effectively for future lessons. You may read the questions aloud to the students.

Lesson 2:   Add and subtract multiples of 100 including counting on to subtract.
Date: 10/23/13

5.A.21

Name _____   Date _____

1. Solve using place value strategies. Use the arrow way or mental math and record your answers. You may use scratch paper if you like.

   a. 2 hundreds 4 tens + 3 hundreds = _____ hundreds _____ tens

                240 + 300 = _____

   b. 340 + 300 = _____   140 + 500 = _____   200 + 440 = _____

   c. 400 + 374 = _____   274 + 500 = _____   700 + 236 = _____

   d. 571 + _____ = 871   ____ + 349 = 749   96 + _____ = 696

   e. _____ + 562 = 862   300 + _____ = 783   600 + _____ = 726

2. Solve using place value strategies. Use the arrow way or mental math and record your answers. You may use scratch paper if you like.

   6 hundreds 2 ones - 4 hundreds = _____ hundreds _____ tens _____ ones
                602 - 400 = _____

   a. 640 - 200 = _____   650 - 300 = _____   750 - _____ = 350

   b. 462 - 200 = _____   667 - 500 = _____   731 - 400 = _____

   c. 431 - _____ = 131   985 - _____ = 585   768 - _____ = 68

   d. _____ - 200 = 662   _____ - 300 = 653   734 - _____ = 234

COMMON CORE | Lesson 2: | Add and subtract multiples of 100 including counting on to subtract.
Date: | 10/23/13

5.A.22

3. Fill in the blank to make true number sentences. Use place value strategies, number bonds, or the arrow way to solve.

   a. 200 more than 389 is _____.

   b. 300 more than _____ is 568.

   c. 400 less than 867 is _____.

   d. _____ less than 962 is 262.

4. Jessica's lemon tree has 526 lemons. She gave away 300 lemons. How many does she have left? Use the arrow way to solve.

Name _____   Date _____

Solve using place value strategies. Use the arrow way or mental math and record your answers. You may use scratch paper if you like.

1. 760 - 500 = _____   880 - 600 = _____   990 - _____ = 590

2. 534 - 334 = _____   _____ - 500 = 356   736 - _____ = 136

Name _____   Date _____

1. Solve using place value strategies. Use the arrow way or mental math and record your answers. You may use scratch paper if you like.

   a. 4 hundreds 5 tens + 2 hundreds = _____ hundreds _____ tens

       450 + 200 = _____

   b. 220 + 300 = _____   230 + 500 = _____   200 + 440 = _____

   c. 400 + 368 = _____   386 + 500 = _____   700 + 239 = _____

   d. 119 + _____ = 519   ____ + 272 = 872   62 + _____ = 562

2. Solve using place value strategies. Use the arrow way or mental math and record your answers. You may use scratch paper if you like.

   5 hundreds 8 ones - 3 hundreds = ____ hundreds ____ tens ____ ones
   508 - 300 = _____

   a. 430 - 200 = _____   550 - 300 = _____   860 - _____ = 360

   b. 628 - 200 = _____   718 - 500 = _____   836 - 400 = _____

   c. 553 - _____ = 153   981 - _____ = 381   827 - _____ = 27

3. Fill in the blank to make true number sentences. Use place value strategies, number bonds, or the arrow way to solve.

a. 300 more than 215 is _____.

b. 300 more than _____ is 668.

c. 500 less than 980 is _____.

d. _____ less than 987 is 487.

e. 600 _____ than 871 is 271.

f. 400 _____ than 444 is 844.

Lesson 3

Objective: Add multiples of 100 and some tens within 1,000.

Suggested Lesson Structure

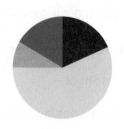

▨ Application Problem	(5 minutes)
▪ Fluency Practice	(11 minutes)
▨ Concept Development	(34 minutes)
▪ Student Debrief	(10 minutes)
Total Time	**(60 minutes)**

Application Problem (5 minutes)

A children's library sold 27 donated books. Now they have 48. How many books were there to begin with?

Note: This problem is a *take from with start unknown*. Because *selling* invites subtraction, the problem may prove to be a challenge for some students. The calculation itself involves using their place value strategies from G2–Module 4, allowing them to choose between using a vertical method, a number bond, or the arrow way.

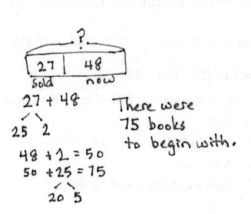

Fluency Practice (11 minutes)

- How Many More to Make 100? **2.NBT.7** (2 minutes)
- Sprint: Adding Multiples of Ten and Some Ones **2.NBT.7** (9 minutes)

How Many More to Make 100? (2 minutes)

Note: Students practice mentally making 100.

- T: How many more ones does 8 need to make 10?
- S: 2 ones.
- T: Say the addition number sentence.
- S: 8 + 2 = 10.
- T: How many more tens does 8 tens need to make 10 tens?
- S: 2 tens.
- T: Say the addition number sentence.

S: 8 tens + 2 tens = 10 tens.

T: How much more does 80 need to make 100?

S: Twenty.

T: Say the addition sentence.

S: 80 + 20 = 100.

Continue with the following sequence: 16, 16 tens and 160, 28, 28 tens and 280.)

Sprint: Adding Multiples of Ten and Some Ones (9 minutes)

Materials: (S) Adding Multiples of Ten and Some Ones Sprint

Note: Students review adding multiples of ten and some ones in preparation for the lesson.

Concept Development (34 minutes)

Materials: (S) Personal white boards, place value chart insert

Problem 1: 420 + 100, 420 + 110

T: (While speaking, record using the arrow way.) 420 + 100 is…?

S: 520.

T: 420 + 100 (pause) + 10 is…?

S: 530.

T: How much did we add in all?

S: 110.

T: Say the complete number sentence for our last problem.

S: 420 + 110 = 530.

T: Turn and talk to your partner about the steps in adding 110 to 420.

S: We first added 1 hundred then 1 ten. → We chopped 110 into two parts, a hundred and a ten and we added each one to make it easier.

$$420 \xrightarrow{+100} 520$$

$$420 \xrightarrow{+100} 520 \xrightarrow{+10} 530$$

First I added 100
Next I added 110

Problem 2: 550 + 200, 550 + 250, 550 + 260

T: Let's try another. (Record as before.) 550 + 200 is…?

S: 750.

T: 550 + 200 (pause) + 50 is…?

S: 800.

T: Add another 10. How many now?

S: 810.

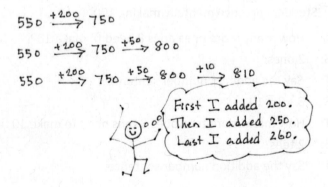

$$550 \xrightarrow{+200} 750$$

$$550 \xrightarrow{+200} 750 \xrightarrow{+50} 800$$

$$550 \xrightarrow{+200} 750 \xrightarrow{+50} 800 \xrightarrow{+10} 810$$

First I added 200.
Then I added 250.
Last I added 260.

COMMON CORE   Lesson 3:   Add multiples of 100 and some tens within 1,000.   5.A.28
                     Date: 10/23/13

T: Talk with your partner. What just happened?

S: We started with 550. We added 200 and then added 50 to make 8 hundred. Then we added 10 more to get 810. → We added 260 in all, one chunk at a time.

Problem 3: 280 + 200, 280 + 220, 280 + 230

T: (Write 280 on the board.)

T: Add 200. How many now?

S: 480.

T: How many more to get to the next hundred? Talk with a partner.

S: Two tens. → Twenty.

T: Now we have 500. Let's show this the arrow way. Do what I do on your boards. (Draw as shown at right.)

S: (Write on their boards.)

T: (Show the same on the board.) We just added 280 + 220. Let's write this using the arrow way. (Write on the board as shown at right.)

T: First we added 200 to 280, and then we added another 20 to compose the new hundred.

T: Now let's add another 10. Show me on your charts.

S: (Add another 10 on charts.)

T: What do we have?

S: 510!

T: This is the same as 280 + 230. First we added 200, then composed a new hundred, and then we added 10 to get 510. Let's show this with the arrow way (shown above right).

Problem 4: 470 + 200, 470 + 210, 470 + 230

In this part, students record their answers on their boards and then turn them over. When most students are ready, say, "Show me." Students hold up their boards for a visual check. Then they erase their boards and get ready for the next problem.

T: 400 + 200. Show me.

S: (Show 600 on their boards.)

T: 470 + 200. Show me.

S: (Show 670 on their boards.)

$$280 \xrightarrow{+200} 480$$
$$280 \xrightarrow{+200} 480 \xrightarrow{+20} 500$$
$$280 \xrightarrow{+200} 480 \xrightarrow{+20} 500 \xrightarrow{+10} 510$$

First I added 200
Next I added 220
Last I added 230

NOTES ON MULTIPLE MEANS OF REPRESENTATION:

For students who struggle to see the change in numbers using the arrow way, use smaller numbers (e.g., 180 + 130 = 310) and couple number sentences with models. Return to a concrete manipulative such as bundled straws to show that 18 tens + 10 tens = 28 tens, or 280. Then ask, "How can I compose a new hundred?" Have students model adding 2 more tens and showing the +20 change using the arrow way. Once they have crossed the hundred, adding the remaining ten is simple.

T: 470 + 210? Talk with a partner first.

S: I added 7 tens and 1 ten to make 8 tens, and then 4 hundreds and 2 hundreds to make 6 hundreds. That's 680. → I added 400 + 200 and then 70 + 10, and 600 plus 80 equals 480. → I used the arrow way and added 200 to 470, which is 670, and then added on 10 more, so 680.

T: Show me.

S: (Show 680 on their boards.)

T: 470 + 230?

S: That's like the problem we did before!

T: Yes! We can find 470 + 230 using 470 + 210 to help us.

MP.6

T: How much more do we need to get from 210 to 230?

S: 20 more.

T: What was 470 + 210?

S: 680!

T: 20 more? (Demonstrate as shown at right.)

S: 700! (Demonstrate as shown at right.)

T: Now try 470 + 250. Talk with your partner about how you solved it.

S: I did 400 + 200 and then did 70 + 30 to get another hundred, and then added the 20 more to get 720. → I added 470 and 200, and then 30 more to get 700, and then the leftover 20 to get 720. → I added 470 + 230 like we did before, and then I just added the last 20.

NOTES ON
MULTIPLE MEANS OF
ACTION AND
EXPRESSION:

Have students talk through their simplifying strategy (i.e., the arrow way) step by step to demonstrate their thinking. Before they solve and discuss, post questions such as those below:

- Which addend did you write first?

- Which did you add first, hundreds or tens? Why?

- How did you show making a new hundred: 3 tens plus 7 tens (e.g., 530 + 70), or 6 tens plus 4 tens (e.g., 860 + 40)?

- When you must cross a hundred, what is it helpful to do first?

$$470 + 200 \qquad 470 \xrightarrow{+200} 670$$
$$470 + 210 \qquad 470 \xrightarrow{+200} 670 \xrightarrow{+10} 680$$
$$470 + 230 \qquad 470 \xrightarrow{+210} 680 \xrightarrow{+20} 700$$

470 + 210 is 10 more than 470 + 200!
470 + 230 is 20 more than 470 + 210!

Problem 5: 590 + 240

T: I notice something interesting about the first number. (Point to 590 on the board.) I wonder if anyone else notices the same thing.

S: It's close to 600! → It's just 10 away from 600. → I can make the next 100 to help me solve the problem.

T: Let's try it. You write what I write. (Record as shown at right.)

$$590 \xrightarrow{+10} 600 \xrightarrow{+30} 630 \xrightarrow{+200} 830$$

T: How much do we have left in 240 after using 10?

S: 230.

Guide students through adding the hundreds and tens the arrow way, asking for their input as you go. When they have worked through this problem, invite them to complete the Problem Set.

Problem Set (10 minutes)

Students should do their personal best to complete the Problem Set within the allotted 10 minutes. For some classes, it may be appropriate to modify the assignment by specifying which problems they work on first. Some problems do not specify a method for solving. Students solve these problems using the RDW approach used for Application Problems.

Student Debrief (10 minutes)

Lesson Objective: Add multiples of 100 and some tens within 1,000.

The Student Debrief is intended to invite reflection and active processing of the total lesson experience.

Invite students to review their solutions for the Problem Set. They should check work by comparing answers with a partner before going over answers as a class. Look for misconceptions or misunderstandings that can be addressed in the Debrief. Guide students in a conversation to debrief the Problem Set and process the lesson.

You may choose to use any combination of the questions below to lead the discussion.

- For Problem 1(b), how does knowing 470 + 400 help you to solve the other problems in that set?

- In Problem 1, what do you notice about the second problem in each set?

- Share with a partner: How did you use the arrow way to solve Problem 1(c), 650 + 280? How did you decompose 280 to add?

- For Problems 2(a) and (b), how did the first problem in each set help you to solve the next two?

- Share with a partner: For Problem 2(c), what was the most efficient way to add 280 + 260? Did you agree or disagree with your partner? Is there more than one way to solve?

- How is thinking about the make ten strategy helpful when composing a new hundred?

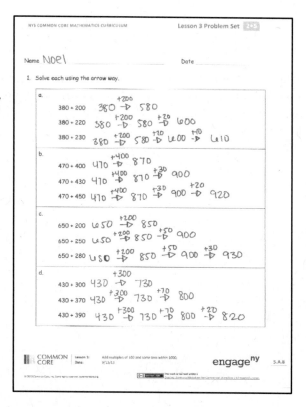

Exit Ticket (3 minutes)

After the Student Debrief, instruct students to complete the Exit Ticket. A review of their work will help you assess the students' understanding of the concepts that were presented in the lesson today and plan more effectively for future lessons. You may read the questions aloud to the students.

A

Correct _____

Add.

1	40 + 3 =		23	45 + 44 =	
2	40 + 8 =		24	44 + 45 =	
3	40 + 9 =		25	30 + 20 =	
4	40 + 10 =		26	34 + 20 =	
5	41 + 10 =		27	34 + 21 =	
6	42 + 10 =		28	34 + 25 =	
7	45 + 10 =		29	34 + 52 =	
8	45 + 11 =		30	50 + 30 =	
9	45 + 12 =		31	56 + 30 =	
10	44 + 12 =		32	56 + 31 =	
11	43 + 12 =		33	56 + 32 =	
12	43 + 13 =		34	32 + 56 =	
13	13 + 43 =		35	23 + 56 =	
14	40 + 20 =		36	24 + 75 =	
15	41 + 20 =		37	16 + 73 =	
16	42 + 20 =		38	34 + 54 =	
17	47 + 20 =		39	62 + 37 =	
18	47 + 30 =		40	45 + 34 =	
19	47 + 40 =		41	27 + 61 =	
20	47 + 41 =		42	16 + 72 =	
21	47 + 42 =		43	36 + 42 =	
22	45 + 42 =		44	32 + 54 =	

© Bill Davidson

COMMON CORE™ | Lesson 3: | Add multiples of 100 and some tens within 1,000.
| Date: | 10/23/13

5.A.33

B

Add.

Improvement _____   # Correct _____

1	50 + 3 =		23	55 + 44 =	
2	50 + 8 =		24	44 + 55 =	
3	50 + 9 =		25	40 + 20 =	
4	50 + 10 =		26	44 + 20 =	
5	51 + 10 =		27	44 + 21 =	
6	52 + 10 =		28	44 + 25 =	
7	55 + 10 =		29	44 + 52 =	
8	55 + 11 =		30	60 + 30 =	
9	55 + 12 =		31	66 + 30 =	
10	54 + 12 =		32	66 + 31 =	
11	53 + 12 =		33	66 + 32 =	
12	53 + 13 =		34	32 + 66 =	
13	13 + 43 =		35	23 + 66 =	
14	50 + 20 =		36	25 + 74 =	
15	51 + 20 =		37	13 + 76 =	
16	52 + 20 =		38	43 + 45 =	
17	57 + 20 =		39	26 + 73 =	
18	57 + 30 =		40	54 + 43 =	
19	57 + 40 =		41	72 + 16 =	
20	57 + 41 =		42	61 + 27 =	
21	57 + 42 =		43	63 + 24 =	
22	55 + 42 =		44	32 + 45 =	

© Bill Davidson

COMMON CORE   Lesson 3:   Add multiples of 100 and some tens within 1,000.
Date: 10/23/13

5.A.34

Name_____   Date _____

1. Solve each using the arrow way.

a.

   380 + 200

   380 + 220

   380 + 230

b.

   470 + 400

   470 + 430

   470 + 450

c.

   650 + 200

   650 + 250

   650 + 280

d.

   430 + 300

   430 + 370

   430 + 390

Lesson 3:	Add multiples of 100 and some tens within 1,000.
Date:	10/23/13

5.A.35

2. Solve using the arrow way or mental math. Use scratch paper if needed.

a. 490 + 200 = _____   210 + 490 = _____   490 + 220 = _____

b. 230 + 700 = _____   230 + 710 = _____   730 + 230 = _____

c. 260 + 240 = _____   260 + 260 = _____   280 + 260 = _____

d. 160 + 150 = _____   370 + 280 = _____   380 + 450 = _____

e. 430 + 290 = _____   660 + 180 = _____   370 + 270 = _____

3. Solve.

a. 66 tens + 20 tens =_____ tens   b. 66 tens + 24 tens =_____ tens

c. 66 tens + 27 tens =_____ tens   d. 67 tens + 28 tens = _____ tens

What is the value of 86 tens? _____

Name _____   Date _____

1. Solve each using the arrow way.

a.

440 + 300

360 + 440

440 + 380

b.

670 + 230

680 + 240

250 + 660

Name _____   Date _____

1. Solve each using the arrow way.

a.
260 + 200
260 + 240
260 + 250
b.
320 + 400
320 + 480
320 + 490
c.
550 + 200
550 + 250
550 + 270
d.
230 + 400
230 + 470
230 + 490

2. Solve using the arrow way or mental math. Use scratch paper if needed.

a. 320 + 200 = _____   280 + 320 = _____   290 + 320 = _____

b. 130 + 500 = _____   130 + 560 = _____   130 + 580 = _____

c. 360 + 240 = _____   350 + 270 = _____   380 + 230 = _____

d. 260 + 250 = _____   270 + 280 = _____   280 + 250 = _____

e. 440 + 280 = _____   660 + 160 = _____   770 + 250 = _____

3. Solve.

a. 34 tens + 20 tens = _____ tens   b. 34 tens + 26 tens = _____ tens

c. 34 tens + 27 tens = _____ tens   d. 34 tens + 28 tens = _____ tens

What is the value of 62 tens? _____

Lesson 4

Objective: Subtract multiples of 100 and some tens within 1,000.

Suggested Lesson Structure

■ Application Problem   (5 minutes)
■ Fluency Practice   (11 minutes)
□ Concept Development   (34 minutes)
■ Student Debrief   (10 minutes)

   Total Time   **(60 minutes)**

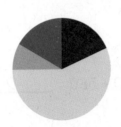

Application Problem (5 minutes)

Diane needs 65 craft sticks to make a gift box. She only has 48. How many more craft sticks does she need?

Note: Instruct students to approach this *addend unknown* problem using any simplifying strategy or even vertical subtraction. When students are finished, invite them to share tape diagrams and solution strategies.

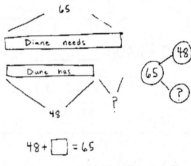

Fluency Practice (11 minutes)

- Subtracting Multiples of Hundreds and Tens **2.NBT.7**   (2 minutes)
- Subtracting Multiples of Ten and Some Ones Sprint **2.NBT.7**   (9 minutes)

Subtracting Multiples of Hundreds and Tens (2 minutes)

Note: Students review fluently subtracting multiples of tens and hundreds in preparation for the lesson.

   T: What is 2 tens less than 130?
   S: 110.
   T: Give the subtraction number sentence.
   S: 130 – 20 = 110.
   T: What is 2 hundreds less than 350?
   S: 150.
   T: Give the subtraction number sentence.
   S: 350 – 200 = 150.

Continue with the following sequence: 6 tens less than 150, 3 hundreds less than 550, 7 tens less than 250.

Subtracting Multiples of Ten and Some Ones Sprint (9 minutes)

Materials: (S) Sprint

Note: Students fluently subtract multiples of ten and some ones in preparation for the lesson.

Concept Development (34 minutes)

Materials: (S) Personal white boards, place value chart insert

Problem 1: 570 – 100, 570 – 110

- T: (While speaking, record using the arrow way.) 570 – 100 is…?
- S: 470.
- T: 570 – 100 (pause) – 10 is?
- S: 460.
- T: How much did we take away in all?
- S: 110.
- T: Say the complete number sentence for our last problem.
- S: 570 – 110 = 460.
- T: Turn and talk to your partner about the steps in subtracting 110 from 570.
- S: We first took away 1 hundred, and then 1 ten. → We made it into two steps: first taking away the hundred, and then the ten, to make it easier.

$$570 \xrightarrow{-100} 470$$
$$570 \xrightarrow{-100} 470 \xrightarrow{-10} 460$$

First I subtracted 100
Then I subtracted 110

Problem 2: 450 – 200, 450 – 210, 450 – 250, 450 – 260

- T: Let's try another. (Record as before.) 450 – 200 is…?
- S: 250.
- T: 450 – 200 (pause) – 10 is…?
- S: 240.
- T: Subtract another 40. How many now?
- S: 200.
- T: Talk with your partner. What just happened?
- S: We started with 450. We took away 200 and then 10 to make 240. Then we took away 40 more to get 200. → We took away 250 in all, one chunk at a time.
- T: What if I needed to solve 450 – 260? Could I use 450 – 250 to help me?
- S: Yes. → They are 10 apart, so it's easy. → Just subtract 10 more.
- T: 450 – 250 – 10 is…?
- S: 190.

$$450 - 250$$
$$450 \xrightarrow{-200} 250 \xrightarrow{-10} 240 \xrightarrow{-40} 200$$

Problem 3: 780 – 300, 780 – 380, 780 – 390

T: Now with your disks, show me 780 – 300.

S: (Students remove 3 hundreds, showing 480 on their place value charts.)

T: (Draw 780 on the board. Cross out 3 hundreds to show 480 on the board.)

T: Yes! Now we have 480. How many do we need to take away from 780 to get 400? Turn and talk.

S: 80 more. → 380 altogether. → Take away 300, then take away 80 more, so 380.

T: I heard some people say we have to take 380 away. Start with 780 and take away 380 with your disks. Do you get 400?

S: Yes!

T: (Cross out 3 hundreds and 8 tens on the board.) I started by taking away 3 hundreds and then 8 tens. I got 400, too.

T: Now I want to solve 780 – 390. What do I need to do to solve this? Turn and talk.

S: Start with 780 – 380, which is 400, then take away 10 more. → Rename a hundred to make 10 tens, and take a ten away. → Do one more step to get 10 less than 400, so 390.

T: I'm going to show this on the board while you do it with your disks. (Unbundle a hundred as shown at right.)

T: What is 780 – 390?

S: 390!

T: Now let's show this problem using the arrow way. (Draw on the board as shown above right.)

Problem 4: 400 – 200, 440 – 200, 440 – 240, 440 – 260

In this part, students record their answers on their personal boards and then turn them over. When most students are ready, say, "Show me." Students hold up their boards for a visual check. Then they erase their boards and get ready for the next problem.

NOTES ON MULTIPLE MEANS OF ENGAGEMENT:

As students show 780 – 390, scaffold questioning to guide connections between the number disks and arrow notation:

- How many hundreds can you subtract first? Which digit changes? Which digit stays the same?

- How many tens do you want to subtract now from 480? Why 80 and not 90?

- Which hundred is closest to 390?

- How much have you subtracted so far? How much is left to subtract from 400?

- What happened to the digits when you subtracted from 400? Why?

- How did you break 390 into smaller parts?

$$780 - 390$$
$$780 \xrightarrow{-300} 480 \xrightarrow{-80} 400 \xrightarrow{-10} 390$$

NOTES ON MULTIPLE MEANS OF ACTION AND EXPRESSION:

Some students may struggle with understanding the sequence from 400 to 200 to 440 – 260:

- Express each number as tens (e.g., 40 – 20, 44 – 20, 44 – 26).

- Then, calculate using tens without including 44 tens – 26 tens (e.g., "What is 44 tens – 22 tens?").

- Restate the first three questions in standard form.

- Include an easier final question, 440 – 250, emphasizing its relationship to 440 – 240.

T:　400 – 200. Show me.

S:　(Show 200 on their boards.)

T:　440 – 200. Show me.

S:　(Show 240 on their boards.)

T:　440 – 240. Show me.

S:　(Show 200 on their boards.)

MP.7

T:　440 – 260? Talk with a partner.

S:　I used 440 – 240 and took away 20
more to get 180. → I did 440 minus 200, then I took away 40 more to make 200, then 20 more. → I took 200 away, then 20, and 20, and 20.

T:　Let's see how we might draw that the arrow way. (Draw as shown at right.)

T:　Now try 620 – 430. Draw it the arrow way.

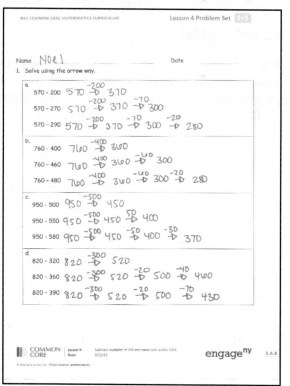

$$440 \xrightarrow{-20} 420 \xrightarrow{-20} 400 \xrightarrow{-20} 380 \xrightarrow{-200} 180$$

$$440 \xrightarrow{-200} 240 \xrightarrow{-40} 200 \xrightarrow{-20} 180$$

$$440 \xrightarrow{-240} 200 \xrightarrow{-20} 180$$

Check student boards and invite several students to share their work on the board.

Problem Set (10 minutes)

Students should do their personal best to complete the Problem Set within the allotted 10 minutes. For some classes, it may be appropriate to modify the assignment by specifying which problems they work on first. Some problems do not specify a method for solving. Students solve these problems using the RDW approach used for Application Problems.

Student Debrief (10 minutes)

Lesson Objective: Subtract multiples of 100 and some tens within 1,000.

The Student Debrief is intended to invite reflection and active processing of the total lesson experience.

Invite students to review their solutions for the Problem Set. They should check work by comparing answers with a partner before going over answers as a class. Look for misconceptions or misunderstandings that can be addressed in the Debrief. Guide students in a conversation to debrief the Problem Set and process the lesson.

You may choose to use any combination of the questions below to lead the discussion.

- For Problem 1(a), how does knowing 540 – 200 help you to solve the other problems in that set?

- For Problem 1(b), what makes solving 760 – 480 more challenging? How did you use what you know about place value to subtract?

NYS COMMON CORE MATHEMATICS CURRICULUM　　　　Lesson 4 Problem Set 2•5

Name Noel　　　　　　　　　Date

1. Solve using the arrow way.

a.

570 – 200　570 $\xrightarrow{-200}$ 370

570 – 270　570 $\xrightarrow{-200}$ 370 $\xrightarrow{-70}$ 300

570 – 290　570 $\xrightarrow{-200}$ 370 $\xrightarrow{-70}$ 300 $\xrightarrow{-20}$ 280

b.

760 – 400　760 $\xrightarrow{-400}$ 360

760 – 460　760 $\xrightarrow{-400}$ 360 $\xrightarrow{-60}$ 300

760 – 480　760 $\xrightarrow{-400}$ 360 $\xrightarrow{-60}$ 300 $\xrightarrow{-20}$ 280

c.

950 – 500　950 $\xrightarrow{-500}$ 450

950 – 550　950 $\xrightarrow{-500}$ 450 $\xrightarrow{-50}$ 400

950 – 580　950 $\xrightarrow{-500}$ 450 $\xrightarrow{-50}$ 400 $\xrightarrow{-30}$ 370

d.

820 – 320　820 $\xrightarrow{-300}$ 520

820 – 360　820 $\xrightarrow{-300}$ 520 $\xrightarrow{-20}$ 500 $\xrightarrow{-40}$ 460

820 – 390　820 $\xrightarrow{-300}$ 520 $\xrightarrow{-20}$ 500 $\xrightarrow{-70}$ 430

COMMON CORE Lesson 4: Subtract multiples of 100 and some tens within 1,000.　engage^ny S.A.8
Date: 9/12/13

- Share with a partner: How did using the arrow way help you to solve Problem 1(c), 950 – 580? What careful observations can you make about the numbers you subtracted? Why did you choose to subtract 50, then 30? Why didn't you just subtract 80?

- Look carefully at the numbers in Problem 1(d). What pattern do you notice within the numbers you subtracted from 820? How did this affect the arrow way? Could you have solved these mentally?

- For Problem 2(d), 740 – 690, Terri solved the problem using an equal sign instead of arrows: 740 – 600 = 140 – 40 = 100 – 50 = 50. Is her answer correct? Is her equation correct? Why can't she use an equal sign to show the change?

- How does using the arrow way help us when there are not enough tens from which to subtract (e.g., 740 – 650)? How did you decompose one part to subtract more easily?

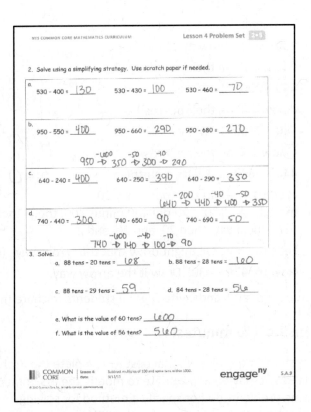

Exit Ticket (3 minutes)

After the Student Debrief, instruct students to complete the Exit Ticket. A review of their work will help you assess the students' understanding of the concepts that were presented in the lesson today and plan more effectively for future lessons. You may read the questions aloud to the students.

A

Subtract.

Correct _____

1	33 - 22 =		23	99 - 32 =	
2	44 - 33 =		24	86 - 32 =	
3	55 - 44 =		25	79 - 32 =	
4	99 - 88 =		26	79 - 23 =	
5	33 - 11 =		27	68 - 13 =	
6	44 - 22 =		28	69 - 23 =	
7	55 - 33 =		29	89 - 14 =	
8	88 - 22 =		30	77 - 12 =	
9	66 - 22 =		31	57 - 12 =	
10	43 - 11 =		32	77 - 32 =	
11	34 - 11 =		33	99 - 36 =	
12	45 - 11 =		34	88 - 25 =	
13	46 - 12 =		35	89 - 36 =	
14	55 - 12 =		36	98 - 16 =	
15	54 - 12 =		37	78 - 26 =	
16	55 - 21 =		38	99 - 37 =	
17	64 - 21 =		39	89 - 38 =	
18	63 - 21 =		40	59 - 28 =	
19	45 - 21 =		41	99 - 58 =	
20	34 - 12 =		42	99 - 45 =	
21	43 - 21 =		43	78 - 43 =	
22	54 - 32 =		44	98 - 73 =	

© Bill Davidson

COMMON CORE | Lesson 4: | Subtract multiples of 100 and some tens within 1,000.
| Date: | 10/23/13

5.A.45

B

Subtract.

Improvement _____　　　　# Correct _____

#			#		
1	33 - 11 =		23	99 - 42 =	
2	44 - 11 =		24	79 - 32 =	
3	55 - 11 =		25	89 - 52 =	
4	88 - 11 =		26	99 - 23 =	
5	33 - 22 =		27	79 - 13 =	
6	44 - 22 =		28	79 - 23 =	
7	55 - 22 =		29	99 - 14 =	
8	99 - 22 =		30	87 - 12 =	
9	77 - 22 =		31	77 - 12 =	
10	34 - 11 =		32	87 - 32 =	
11	43 - 11 =		33	99 - 36 =	
12	54 - 11 =		34	78 - 25 =	
13	55 - 12 =		35	79 - 36 =	
14	46 - 12 =		36	88 - 16 =	
15	44 - 12 =		37	88 - 26 =	
16	64 21 =		38	89 - 37 =	
17	55 - 21 =		39	99 - 38 =	
18	53 - 21 =		40	69 - 28 =	
19	44 - 21 =		41	89 - 58 =	
20	34 - 22 =		42	99 - 45 =	
21	43 - 22 =		43	68 - 43 =	
22	54 - 22 =		44	98 - 72 =	

© Bill Davidson

Name _____   Date _____

1. Solve using the arrow way.

a.

570 – 200

570 – 270

570 – 290

b.

760 – 400

760 – 460

760 – 480

c.

950 - 500

950 - 550

950 - 580

d.

820 – 320

820 – 360

820 – 390

2. Solve using a simplifying strategy. Use scratch paper if needed.

a.

530 – 400 = _____   530 – 430 = _____   530 – 460 = _____

b.

950 - 550 = _____   950 - 660 = _____   950 - 680 = _____

c.

640 - 240 = _____   640 - 250 = _____   640 - 290 = _____

d.

740 - 440 = _____   740 - 650 = _____   740 - 690 = _____

3. Solve.

a. 88 tens – 20 tens = _____   b. 88 tens – 28 tens = _____

c. 88 tens – 29 tens = _____   d. 84 tens – 28 tens = _____

e. What is the value of 60 tens? _____

f. What is the value of 56 tens? _____

Name _____   Date _____

1. Solve using a simplifying strategy. Show your work if needed.

    830 - 530 = _____   830 - 750 = _____   830 - 780 = _____

    Solve.

    a. 67 tens – 30 tens = _____ tens. The value is _____.

    b. 67 tens – 37 tens = _____ tens. The value is _____.

    c. 67 tens – 39 tens = _____ tens. The value is _____.

Name _____   Date _____

1. Solve using the arrow way.

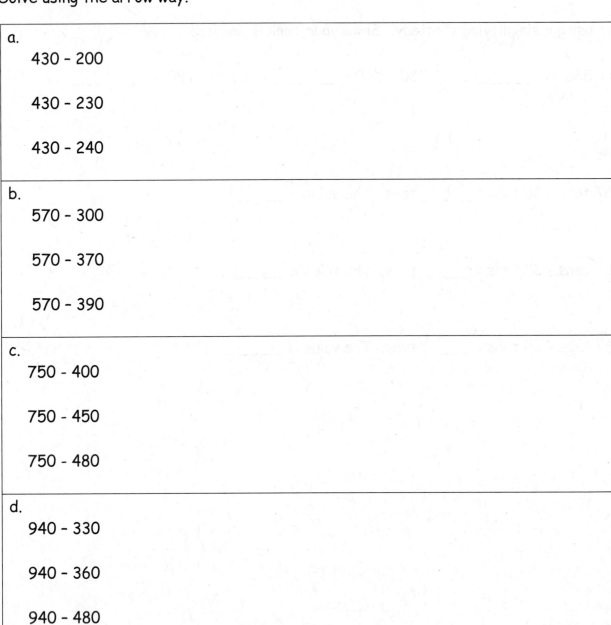

a.

430 – 200

430 – 230

430 – 240

b.

570 – 300

570 – 370

570 – 390

c.

750 - 400

750 - 450

750 - 480

d.

940 – 330

940 – 360

940 – 480

2. Solve using a simplifying strategy. Use scratch paper if needed.

a.

330 – 200 = _____   330 – 230 = _____   330 – 260 = _____

b.

440 - 240 = _____   440 - 260 = _____   440 - 290 = _____

c.

860 - 560 = _____   860 - 570 = _____   860 - 590 = _____

d.

970 - 470 = _____   970 - 480 = _____   970 - 490 = _____

3. Solve.

a. 66 tens – 30 tens = _____   b. 66 tens – 36 tens = _____

c. 66 tens – 38 tens = _____   d. 67 tens – 39 tens = _____

e. What is the value of 28 tens? _____

f. What is the value of 36 tens? _____

Lesson 5

Objective: Use the associative property to make a hundred in one addend.

Suggested Lesson Structure

▨ Application Problem	(6 minutes)
■ Fluency Practice	(10 minutes)
▤ Concept Development	(34 minutes)
▨ Student Debrief	(10 minutes)
Total Time	**(60 minutes)**

Application Problem (6 minutes)

Jenny had 39 collectible cards in her collection. Tammy gave her 36 more. How many collectible cards does Jenny have now?

Note: This problem is designed to provide a real life context for the skills the students have learned in this lesson and in the previous ones. Invite students to solve this problem using number bonds or any other simplifying strategy they have learned. After solving the problem, have students share their strategies with a partner.

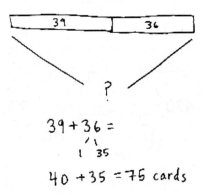

Fluency Practice (10 minutes)

- Making the Next Hundred **2.NBT.5, 2.NBT.7**   (4 minutes)
- Making the Next Hundred to Add **2.NBT.5, 2.NBT.7**   (6 minutes)

Making the Next Hundred (4 minutes)

Note: This fluency will review foundations that lead into today's lesson.

T: (Post 170 + ___ = 200 on the board.) Let's find missing parts to make the next ten. If I say 170, you would say 30. Ready? 170.

S: 30.

T: Give the number sentence.

S: 170 + 30 = 200.

Continue with the following possible sequence: 190, 160, 260, 270, 370, 380, 580, 620, 720, 740, 940, 194,

Lesson 5:	Use the associative property to make a hundred in one addend.	
Date:	10/23/13	5.A.52

196, 216, 214, 224.

Making the Next Hundred to Add (6 minutes)

Note: This fluency will review foundations that lead into today's lesson.

Post on board:

T: When I say 9 tens + 4 tens, you say 10 tens + 3 tens. Ready? 9 tens + 4 tens.

$90 + 40 =$ _____

S: 10 tens + 3 tens.

$\wedge$

T: Answer.

10   30

S: 130.

$100 + 30 =$

T: 90 + 40.

S: 130.

Continue with possible sequence: 19 tens + 4 tens, 29 tens + 4 tens, 29 tens + 14 tens, 9 tens + 6 tens, 19 tens + 6 tens, 19 tens + 16 tens, 29 tens + 16 tens, 8 tens + 3 tens, 18 tens + 3 tens, 18 tens + 13 tens, 28 tens + 13 tens, 8 tens + 5 tens, 18 tens + 15 tens, 28 tens + 15 tens.

Concept Development (34 minutes)

Materials: (S) Personal white boards

Problem Set 1: 17 + 13, 17 tens + 13 tens, 170 + 130, 170 + 40

T: What is 17 + 12?

S: 29!

T: What is 17 + 13?

S: 30!

T: That was fast! How did you know?

S: I added 1 more to 17 + 12. → 13 is 1 more than 12, so the answer had to be 1 more than 29.

T: How many tens equal 17 tens plus 13 tens?

S: 30 tens.

T: What is the value of 30 tens?

S: 300!

T: What is 170 + 130?

S: 300.

T: What happened when we added those numbers? Turn and talk.

S: We made a new hundred, just like when we added 17 to 13 and made a new ten. → We composed a new hundred. → Instead of 30 ones, we have 30 tens. It's just like 17 + 13 except that the place value is different.

T: What is 17 + 14? Write it on your board and turn it over so I know when you're ready.

T: (Wait until students are ready.) Show me!

S:　31!

T:　How many tens equal 17 tens plus 14 tens?

S:　31 tens!

T:　170 + 140?

S:　310!

T:　Talk with your partner. How did you know?

S:　17 tens plus 14 tens is just like 17 + 14, only in tens, so the answer is similar but in tens. → 170 + 140 is 10 more than 170 + 130, so the answer has to be 10 more. → Since 170 + 130 was 30 tens, I knew that 170 + 140 had to be 31 tens; it's 1 more ten.

Extend to 17 tens + 15 tens and continue until students are comfortable with the concept.

NOTES ON MULTIPLE MEANS OF ACTION AND EXPRESSION:

For accelerated learners, ask for alternative addition and subtraction number sentences that would have the same total (e.g., 32 tens or 320). Include number sentences with three addends.

- ____ + ____ = 32 tens
- 32 tens - ____ = ____
- ____ + ____ + ____ = 320

Problem Set 2: Add multiples of 10 by making a hundred.

T:　In the past, we've used number bonds to make the next ten. Let's do it here, too, to make our adding easier when we have hundreds.

T:　(Write 190 + 120 on the board.) Is one of these numbers close to the next hundred?

S:　Yes!

T:　Which one?

S:　190!

T:　What is it close to?

S:　200!

T:　How many more do we need to make 200?

S:　10 more!

T:　Where can we get 10 more?

S:　From the 120!

T:　Great idea! Let's break apart 120 into 110 and 10. Now, we can add the 10 from 120 to the 190. And we know that 190 plus 10 equals 200. (Show number bond on the board.)

T:　What is our new addition problem? (Point to corresponding parts of the number bond.)

S:　200 + 110!

T:　Talk with a partner. What does this equal?

$$190 + 120$$

$$190 + 10 = 200$$
$$200 + 110 = 310$$

NOTES ON MULTIPLE MEANS OF REPRESENTATION:

For students who have trouble seeing that the two expressions, 190 + 120 and 200 + 110, are equivalent, show compensation using manipulatives, such as place value disks.

S:　310! → I did 200 + 100 and added 10, so 310. → I remembered what we did with tens, so I thought of 20 + 11, which is 31, and 31 tens equals 310.

T:　I heard someone say they remembered what they did with the tens. Great! When we have a zero in the ones place, we can think of it as tens.

Lesson 5:　Use the associative property to make a hundred in one addend.
Date:　　　10/23/13

5.A.54

T: How can we prove that 200 + 110 is the same as 190 + 120? Turn and talk.

S: I can add 100 to 190 and get 290, then count 20 more by tens, so 300, 310. → I can show both the arrow way, first adding hundreds, then tens. → I just know that since 190 is 10 less than 200, the other part has to be 10 more than 110. Then the total will be equal. → I did it by using the algorithm, and I got the same answer.

Have students solve the following problems on their personal boards with a partner using number bonds:
190 + 160, 430 + 180, 370 + 240.

Problem Set 3: Add three-digit numbers by making a hundred.

T: So far, we've only been working with numbers that have zero in the ones place. Let's try something different now. (Write 199 + 25 on the board.)

T: What hundred is close to 199?

S: 200!

T: How far away is it?

S: 1 away!

T: Let's try decomposing 25 into 24 and 1. We can add the 1 from 25 to the 199. And we know that 199 plus 1 equals 200. (Draw number bond.) What is our new addition problem?

S: 200 + 24!

T: And what is the total?

S: 224!

MP.7 T: Let's try another example. (Write 295 + 78 on the board.)

$$199 + 25$$
$$1 \diagup \diagdown 24$$
$$199 + 1 = 200$$
$$200 + 24 = 224$$

T: I see one number that is close to some hundreds. Which number is that?

S: 295!

T: How far away is it?

S: 5 away!

T: Talk with a partner. How would you use a number bond to make a new, simpler number sentence?

S: I could make 295 into 300 and have 73 left over. → I break 78 into 5 and 73, and then I give the 5 to 295, so 300 + 73. → I get 300 and 73.

T: (After student conversation, choose a volunteer to show the number bond and new number sentence on the board.) What is 300 + 73?

S: 373!

T: Now let's try one that has hundreds in both. (Write 535 + 397 on the board.)

T: Which number is closer to the next hundred?

S: 397!

T: With a partner, write the number bond and new addition problem. Then, solve it.

MP.7

S: I made 532 + 400, so 932. → 397 is 3 away from 400, so I need to move 3 from the 535 to the 597. 400 + 532 = 932. → Since I added 3 to 397, I had to take away 3 from 535. Now it's easy to add 4 hundreds onto 532.

Have students solve the following problems on their personal boards with a partner using number bonds: 299 + 22, 495 + 30, 527 + 296. As they complete the problems, they may begin work on the Problem Set.

Problem Set (10 minutes)

Students should do their personal best to complete the Problem Set within the allotted 10 minutes. For some classes, it may be appropriate to modify the assignment by specifying which problems they work on first. Some problems do not specify a method for solving. Students solve these problems using the RDW approach used for Application Problems.

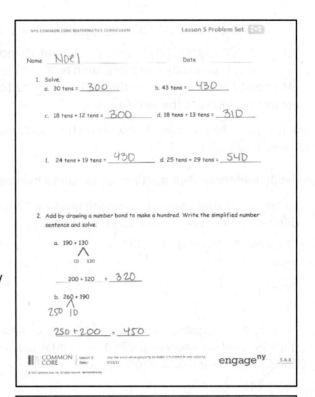

Student Debrief (10 minutes)

Lesson Objective: Use the associative property to make a hundred in one addend.

The Student Debrief is intended to invite reflection and active processing of the total lesson experience.

Invite students to review their solutions for the Problem Set. They should check work by comparing answers with a partner before going over answers as a class. Look for misconceptions or misunderstandings that can be addressed in the Debrief. Guide students in a conversation to debrief the Problem Set and process the lesson.

You may choose to use any combination of the questions below to lead the discussion.

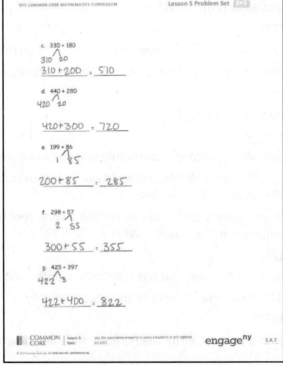

- For Problem 1(a), 18 tens + 12 tens is the same as adding what two numbers? What is the value of 30 tens? How does (a) help you to solve (b)?

- Share with a partner: How did you solve Problem 1(c)? How could you have used 1(c) to help you solve (d)? What would it look like to solve with a number bond?

COMMON CORE™ | Lesson 5: | Use the associative property to make a hundred in one addend.
           | Date: | 10/23/13   **5.A.56**

- In Problem 2(b), 260 + 190, how did you use a number bond to make a new, simpler addition problem? Which number did you break apart, or decompose? Why?

- In Problem 2(c), 330 + 180, how did you extend your understanding of the make ten strategy? What do these strategies have in common? What is 330 + 180 the Say Ten way?

- For Problem 2(e), 199 + 86, can you think of alternate strategies to solve? Do you think you could use disks and a place value chart? Why should we choose a number bond? Explain to your partner the steps you took to solve.

- What connections can you make between the number bond strategy and the arrow way? What is the goal of these strategies?

Exit Ticket (3 minutes)

After the Student Debrief, instruct students to complete the Exit Ticket. A review of their work will help you assess the students' understanding of the concepts that were presented in the lesson today and plan more effectively for future lessons. You may read the questions aloud to the students.

COMMON CORE™

Lesson 5:   Use the associative property to make a hundred in one addend.
Date: 10/23/13

5.A.57

Name _____   Date _____

1. Solve.

   a. 30 tens = _____   b. 43 tens = _____

   c. 18 tens + 12 tens = _____   d. 18 tens + 13 tens = _____

   e. 24 tens + 19 tens = _____   f. 25 tens + 29 tens = _____

2. Add by drawing a number bond to make a hundred. Write the simplified number sentence and solve.

   a. 190 + 130

   10   120

   _____200 + 120_____ = _____

   b. 260 + 190

   _____ = _____

   c. 330 + 180

   _____ = _____

Lesson 5:   Use the associative property to make a hundred in one addend.
Date: 10/23/13

5.A.58

d. 440 + 280

_____ = _____

e. 199 + 86

_____ = _____

f. 298 + 57

_____ = _____

g. 425 + 397

_____ = _____

COMMON
CORE™

Lesson 5:   Use the associative property to make a hundred in one addend.
Date: 10/23/13

5.A.59

Name _____   Date _____

Add by drawing a number bond to make a hundred. Write the simplified number sentence and solve.

1.
    a. 390 + 210

      _____ = _____

    b. 798 + 57

      _____ = _____

Solve.

2. 53 tens + 38 tens = _____

COMMON CORE™

Lesson 5:   Use the associative property to make a hundred in one addend.

Date: 10/23/13

5.A.60

Name _____ Date _____

1. Solve.

   a. 32 tens = _____

   b. 52 tens = _____

   c. 19 tens + 11 tens = _____

   d. 19 tens + 13 tens = _____

   e. 28 tens + 23 tens = _____

   f. 28 tens + 24 tens = _____

2. Add by drawing a number bond to make a hundred. Write the simplified number sentence and solve.

   a. 90 + 180

      10   170

      ___100 + 170___ = _____

   b. 190 + 460

      _____ = _____

COMMON CORE™

Lesson 5:   Use the associative property to make a hundred in one addend.
Date: 10/23/13

5.A.61

c. 540 + 280

_____ = _____

d. 380 + 430

_____ = _____

e. 99 + 141

_____ = _____

f. 75 + 299

_____ = _____

g. 795 + 156

_____ = _____

 Lesson 5:   Use the associative property to make a hundred in one addend.
Date: 10/23/13

5.A.62

Lesson 6

Objective: Use the associative property to subtract from three-digit numbers and verify solutions with addition.

Suggested Lesson Structure

■ Application Problems   (5 minutes)
■ Fluency Practice   (9 minutes)
■ Concept Development   (36 minutes)
■ Student Debrief   (10 minutes)
   Total Time   **(60 minutes)**

Application Problem (5 minutes)

Maria made 60 cupcakes for the school bake sale. She sold 28 cupcakes on the first day. How many cupcakes did she have left?

Note: This Application Problem primes students to subtract multiples of 10. They may use whichever subtraction strategy they prefer. Lead students through the RDW process, or have students work independently and then share their work.

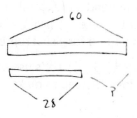

$60 - 28 = 32$ cupcakes

$60 \xrightarrow{-20} 40 \xrightarrow{-8} 32$

Fluency Practice (9 minutes)

- Compensation with Linking Cubes **2.NBT.5**   (5 minutes)
- Compensation with Subtraction **2.NBT.5**   (4 minutes)

Compensation with Linking Cubes (5 minutes)

Materials: (S) Linking cubes in three colors

Note: This is a teacher directed, whole class activity. With continued practice, students will gain automaticity compensating when subtracting.

T: Show a row of 8 cubes with five in yellow and 3 in red and a row of 5 yellow cubes.

T: What is the difference between 8 and 5?

S: 3.

T: What is a number sentence to represent the difference?

$8 - 5 = 9 - 6$

Lesson 6:   Use the associative property to subtract from three-digit numbers and
            verify solutions with addition.
Date: 10/23/13

5.A.63

S: 8 – 5 = 3.

T: Now add 1 green cube to the end of each stick. Has the difference changed?

S: No.

T: What is the new number sentence?

S: 9 – 6 = 3.

T: True or false? (Write 8 – 5 = 9 – 6 on the board.)

S: True.

Continue with possible sequence: 7 – 3 = 8 – 4, 9 – 4 = 10 – 5.

NOTES ON MULTIPLE MEANS OF ENGAGEMENT:

Cultivate confidence, particularly for students who shy away from participating. Invite a student forward to add 1 green cube to the end of each stick. Guide her to give the new number sentence, pointing to cubes as she speaks. Then, during pair-share, have a private conversation: "What does this mean?" Listen intently to see if the student understands that the difference does not change. Celebrate risk taking and problem solving!

Compensation with Subtraction (4 minutes)

Note: This fluency drill prepares students for the lesson by reviewing compensation when subtracting. Students add the same amount to the minuend and subtrahend to make a multiple of 10 in order to make the problem easier to solve. Post a tape diagram on board for visual representation.

T: (Write 34 – 19 = _____.) Let's use the same mental math strategy to subtract larger numbers. How much more does 19 need to make the next ten?

S: 1 more.

T: Add 1 to each number and give me the number sentence.

+ 1	34

+ 1	19

S: 35 – 20 = 15.

T: 34 – 19 is...?

S: 15.

T: True or false? (Write 34 – 19 = 35 – 20 on board.)

S: True.

T: What are both expressions equal to?

S: 15.

T: 43 – 28.

S: 45 – 30 = 15.

Continue with the following possible sequence: 52 – 29, 64 – 38, 83 – 27, 74 – 49, 93 – 47, 95 – 58.

Concept Development (36 minutes)

Materials: (T) Linking cubes in three colors (S) Personal white boards

Note: Compensation for subtraction is always shown on the left-hand side, whether you are manipulating linking cubes or drawing a tape diagram, in order to make it clear that the difference remains the same. If compensation is shown on the right, the difference shifts, so students may wonder if it has changed.

Lesson 6:	Use the associative property to subtract from three-digit numbers and verify solutions with addition.
Date:	10/23/13

5.A.64

Problem 1: Compensation with two-digit numbers and checking with addition.

T: Let's imagine each of the cubes is worth 10. (Show the 8 and 5 sticks.) Let's count them by tens. (Count together: 10, 20, 30, etc.)

T: What is the difference now? Say the number sentence.

S: 80 – 50 = 30.

T: (Add 1 cube to the end of each stick.) How about now?

S: 90 – 60 = 30.

T: (Draw a two-bar diagram to represent these two problems.)

T: Let's check to see if that worked for both of these problems. (Point to 80 – 50.) In this problem, since 80 is the whole, and 50 is one part, what is the other part? (Point to the 30.)

S: 30!

T: We know if we add both parts, we should get the whole again. Does it work? If we add 30 to 50, what do we get?

S: 80!

T: It works! (Write 30 + 50 = 80 on the board.)

Repeat this sequence with 90 – 60 = 30.

T: (Quickly draw the bonds as exemplified to the right.) Both bonds have the same missing part!

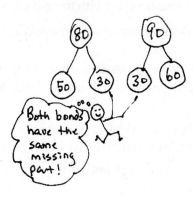

Problem 2: Compensation with multiples of 10 and three-digit numbers and checking with addition.

T: Let's try a new problem. (Write 230 – 180 on the board.)

T: This problem is a bit challenging, isn't it?

T: What is 250 – 200?

S: 50!

T: How did you know that so fast?

S: Because the hundreds were the same, so 50 is left. → It's easy! Just take away 200. → I started at 200, and 50 more is 250, so the answer is 50.

T: It's easier to take away the hundreds, isn't it?

Draw a tape diagram on the board to represent 230 – 180. Direct students to do the same. Call a student volunteer forward to label the tape diagram.

T: Can you tell me how 230 – 180 and my other problem, 250 – 200, are related? Turn and talk.

S: 230 – 180 is the same as 250 – 200, but you added 20 more to each number. → The difference is the same, 50. → Even though the number sentence is different, they are equal to each other.

T: (Call a volunteer to add 20 to each bar on the board to change the model to 250 – 200.)

S: (Do the same at their seats.)

Lesson 6: Use the associative property to subtract from three-digit numbers and verify solutions with addition.

Date: 10/23/13

5.A.65

MP.7

T: Now how much is each bar worth?

S: The top bar is 250, and the bottom bar is 200.

T: We added 20 to each bar to make the problem easy!

T: Now let's check it with addition the way we did before. (Point and talk.) What is 50 + 200?

S: 250!

T: What is 50 + 180? (Give students a moment to think.)

S: 230.

T: How do you know? Talk with a partner.

S: The parts go together to make the same whole. → I counted by tens just to make sure. → It's like a number bond, so the subtraction and addition problems are related.

T: (Write on the board: 330 – 280, 500 – 370, 570 – 380.) Now, it's your turn. On your board, solve these problems by using this strategy.

NOTES ON
MULTIPLE MEANS OF
ACTION AND
EXPRESSION:

Some students may struggle to see the compensation. Allow them to continue using the linking cubes to represent the larger numbers. Again, instruct them to show the compensation with an alternate color.

For students struggling with fine motor skills, provide square tiles to help them draw the tape diagrams. Do not, however, become overly concerned with precision, as their conceptual understanding is paramount. The tape diagram is a vehicle for understanding the compensation.

Problem 3: Compensation with three-digit numbers and checking with addition.

T: So far, we have only been working with numbers with zero ones. Now let's try subtracting numbers with some ones.

T: (Write 321 – 199 on the board.) In this problem, I see that the number I am taking away is very close to 200. How many more do I need to add to make 200?

S: 1!

T: Let's draw a tape diagram for that. (Draw a tape diagram representing 321 – 199 and add 1 to the left of each bar.) You write this on your board, too.

T: What is our new problem?

S: 322 – 200!

T: That's easier, don't you think? Turn your board over when you have the answer.

T: What is 322 – 200?

S: 122!

T: Let's check that with addition. (Write 122 + 200 on the board.) What is this?

S: 322!

T: It works! Let's try another problem. (Write 514 – 290 on the board below a tape diagram.)

T: How much should we add to make this problem easier?

S: 10!

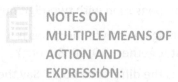

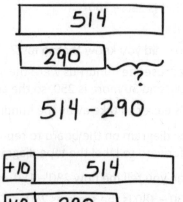

COMMON
CORE™

Lesson 6:   Use the associative property to subtract from three-digit numbers and verify solutions with addition.
Date: 10/23/13

5.A.66

T: What is our new problem? (Draw 10 more onto the left of each bar.)

S;   524 – 200!

T: Draw a tape diagram and solve. Check your answer using addition.

Repeat with the following problems: 547 – 498, 720 – 575.

Problem Set (10 minutes)

Students should do their personal best to complete the Problem Set within the allotted 10 minutes. For some classes, it may be appropriate to modify the assignment by specifying which problems they work on first. Some problems do not specify a method for solving. Students solve these problems using the RDW approach used for Application Problems.

Student Debrief (10 minutes)

Lesson Objective: Use the associative property to subtract from three-digit numbers and verify solutions with addition.

The Student Debrief is intended to invite reflection and active processing of the total lesson experience.

Invite students to review their solutions for the Problem Set. They should check work by comparing answers with a partner before going over answers as a class. Look for misconceptions or misunderstandings that can be addressed in the Debrief. Guide students in a conversation to debrief the Problem Set and process the lesson.

You may choose to use any combination of the questions below to lead the discussion.

- In Problem 1(b), 320 - 190, what number did you add to both numbers in the equation to make an easier problem? Why? How did you check your work?

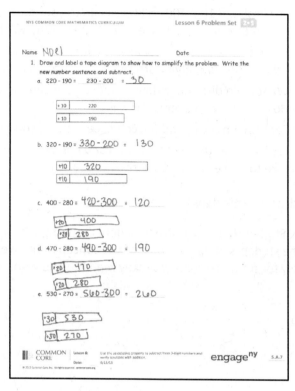

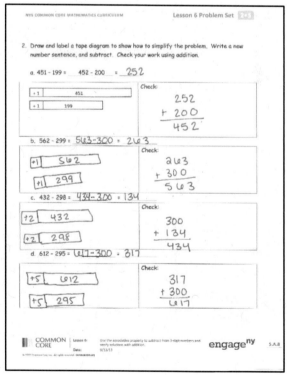

COMMON CORE™ | Lesson 6:   Use the associative property to subtract from three-digit numbers and verify solutions with addition.

Date: 10/23/13

5.A.67

- For Problem 1(c), 400 – 280, explain to your partner your strategy to solve. Then, compare how you checked your work. Make a prediction: Why will this be easier than using the algorithm to solve?

- Share with a partner: What was your new number sentence for Problem 1(e)? What is the solution? What other simplifying strategies could you use to check your work?

- What main difference do you notice between the problems on pages 1 and 2 of the Problem Set? How are they different? How is your goal the same?

- For Problems 1(b) and (c), convince me that compensation is a smart strategy to select.

- Explain what the compensation and number bond strategies have in common. What actions to you take to make solving easier?

Exit Ticket (3 minutes)

After the Student Debrief, instruct students to complete the Exit Ticket. A review of their work will help you assess the students' understanding of the concepts that were presented in the lesson today and plan more effectively for future lessons. You may read the questions aloud to the students.

COMMON CORE™ | Lesson 6:   Use the associative property to subtract from three-digit numbers and verify solutions with addition.
Date: 10/23/13

5.A.68

Name _____   Date _____

1. Draw and label a tape diagram to show how to simplify the problem. Write the new number sentence, and then subtract.

   a. 220 – 190 = ___230 – 200___ = _____

+ 10	220
+ 10	190

   b. 320 – 190 = _____ = _____

   c. 400 – 280 = _____ = _____

   d. 470 – 280 = _____ = _____

   e. 530 – 270 = _____ = _____

COMMON
CORE™

Lesson 6:   Use the associative property to subtract from three-digit numbers and
              verify solutions with addition.
Date: 10/23/13

5.A.69

2. Draw and label a tape diagram to show how to simplify the problem. Write a new number sentence, and then subtract. Check your work using addition.

a. 451 – 199 = ____452 – 200____ = _____

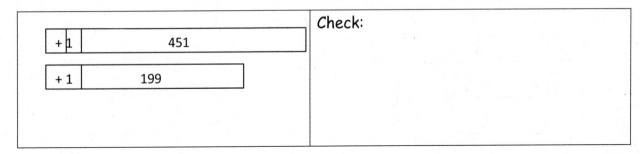

Check:

b. 562 – 299 = _____ = _____

Check:

c. 432 – 298 = _____ = _____

Check:

d. 612 – 295 = _____ = _____

Check:

COMMON CORE™   Lesson 6:   Use the associative property to subtract from three-digit numbers and verify solutions with addition.   Date: 10/23/13   5.A.70

© 2013 Common Core, Inc. All rights reserved. **commoncore.org**

Name _____   Date _____

Draw and label a tape diagram to show how to simplify the problem. Write the new number sentence, and then subtract.

1. 363 – 198 = _____ = _____

2. 671 – 399 = _____ = _____

3. 862 – 490 = _____ = _____

COMMON CORE™   Lesson 6:   Use the associative property to subtract from three-digit numbers and verify solutions with addition.
Date: 10/23/13

5.A.71

Name _____   Date _____

1. Draw and label a tape diagram to show how to simplify the problem. Write the new
    number sentence, and then subtract.

    a. 340 – 190 = ___350 – 200___ = _____

+ 10	340

+ 10	190

    b. 420 – 190 = _____ = _____

    c. 500 – 280 = _____ = _____

    d. 650 – 280 = _____ = _____

    e. 740 – 270 = _____ = _____

COMMON CORE™   Lesson 6:   Use the associative property to subtract from three-digit numbers and verify solutions with addition.
Date: 10/23/13

5.A.72

2. Draw and label a tape diagram to show how to simplify the problem. Write a new number sentence, and then subtract. Check your work using addition.

a. 236 – 99 = ____237 - 100____ = _____

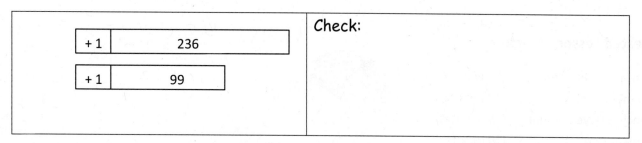

	Check:

b. 372 – 199 = _____ = _____

	Check:

c. 442 – 298 = _____ = _____

	Check:

d. 718 – 390 = _____ = _____

	Check:

COMMON CORE™ | Lesson 6:   Use the associative property to subtract from three-digit numbers and
                     | verify solutions with addition.
                     | **Date:**   10/23/13

5.A.73

© 2013 Common Core, Inc. All rights reserved. **commoncore.org**

Lesson 7

Objective: Share and critique strategies for varied addition and subtraction problems within 1,000.

Suggested Lesson Structure

▨	Application Problem	(5 minutes)
■	Fluency Practice	(10 minutes)
▨	Concept Development	(35 minutes)
■	Student Debrief	(10 minutes)
	Total Time	**(60 minutes)**

Application Problem (5 minutes)

Jeannie got a pedometer to count her steps. The first hour, she walked 43 steps. The next hour, she walked 48 steps.

a. How many steps did she walk in the first two hours?

b. How many more steps did she walk in the second hour than in the first?

Note: This problem invites students to apply strategies from the previous lessons. They may work alone or with partners. Guide struggling students in drawing tape diagrams to represent the problem, especially for the second step. Encourage the students to explain their thinking about why they used the strategy they chose.

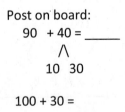

a)

$43 + 48 = 91 \text{ steps}$

41 2

$50 + 41 = 91 \text{ steps}$

b) 1st hour

2nd hour

$43 + 5 = 48$

5 more steps

Fluency Practice (10 minutes)

- Making the Next Hundred to Add **2.NBT.5, 2.NBT.7**   (5 minutes)
- Compensation with Subtraction **2.NBT.5**   (5 minutes)

Making the Next Hundred to Add (5 minutes)

Note: This fluency will review foundations that lead into today's lesson.

  T: When I say, 9 tens + 4 tens, you say 10 tens + 3 tens.
      Ready? 9 tens + 4 tens.

  S: 10 tens + 3 tens.

Post on board:

$90 + 40 =$ _____

$\wedge$

10   30

$100 + 30 =$

T: Answer.

S: 130.

T: 90 + 40.

S: 130.

Continue with this possible sequence: 19 tens + 4 tens, 29 tens + 4 tens, 29 tens + 14 tens, 9 tens + 6 tens, 19 tens + 6 tens, 19 tens + 16 tens, 29 tens + 16 tens, 8 tens + 3 tens, 18 tens + 3 tens, 18 tens + 13 tens, 28 tens + 13 tens, 8 tens + 5 tens, 18 tens + 15 tens, 28 tens + 15 tens.

Compensation with Subtraction (5 minutes)

Note: This fluency drill prepares students for the lesson by reviewing compensation when subtracting. Students add the same amount to the minuend and subtrahend to make a multiple of 10 thus making the problem easier to solve. Post the tape diagram on the board for visual representation.

T: (Write 34 – 19 = _____.) Let's use a mental math strategy to subtract. What needs to be added to 19 to make the next ten?

S: 1 more.

T: Add 1 to each number and give me the number sentence.

| + 1 | 34 |
| + 1 | 19 |

S: 35 – 20 = 15.

T: 34 – 19 is...?

S: 15.

T: True or false? (Write 34 – 19 = 35 – 20 on board.)

S: True.

T: What are both expressions equal to?

S: 15.

T: 43 – 28.

S: 45 – 30 = 15.

Continue with the following possible sequence: 52 – 29, 64 – 38, 83 – 27, 74 – 49, 93 – 47, 95 – 58.

Concept Development (35 minutes)

Materials: (T) Student work samples (S) Personal white boards

Problem 1: 697 + 223

T: (Project and read.) The problem is 697 + 223. Turn and talk to your partner about how you would solve this problem.

T: (Project Student A's sample.) How did Student A solve this problem? Explain to your partner what this student was thinking. What strategy did Student A

NOTES ON
MULTIPLE MEANS OF
ENGAGEMENT:

For struggling students, assign a buddy who will clarify processes and who can comfortably evaluate student work samples. As some students model their higher-level thinking, they unknowingly encourage their buddies to make connections between problem-solving strategies.

| Lesson 7: | Share and critique strategies for varied addition and subtraction problems within 1,000. |
| Date: | 10/23/13 |

5.A.75

use?

S: She used number bonds to make a new hundred. → She made 700 + 220 to get 920. → She was thinking that she could easily make a hundred because 697 is only 3 away from 700.

T: (Label student work *Number bond strategy*.)

T: Let's look at a different way to solve this. (Project Student B's work.)

MP.3

T: What did Student B choose to do? Turn and talk.

S: He used the arrow way. → First he used arrows to make a new hundred, and then he added the hundreds and tens.

T: (Label student work *Arrow way*.)

T: Which way would you do it? Discuss with your partner.

S: I would use the number bonds, because it's so easy to add the hundreds after that. → The arrow helps me make sure I don't miss any parts of the number.

T: Both work. For this one I would use the bonds. It's fewer steps, and I'm always looking for the shortest route!

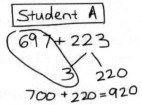

Problem 2: 864 – 380

T: (Project and read the problem.) How would you solve this problem? Solve it on your personal board and discuss it with a partner.

S: (Circulate and listen while students solve and discuss.)

T: (Project the work samples from Students C and D.) Let's see how these two students solved the problem. One is correct, and one is incorrect. Which is which, and why? Discuss it with a partner.

S: Student C used a number bond, but he did it wrong. He added 20 to 380, but he took 20 away from 864!
→ That means the numbers got closer. The difference changed. Student D kept the difference the same.
→ The second one is right. When you add the same number to both numbers, the difference stays the same. The first one gave us the wrong answer.

T: I even see grown ups make this mistake!! To keep the difference the same, we have to do the same thing to both numbers when we subtract.

Student C

864 – 380

844 20

844 – 400 = 444

Student D

|+20| 864 |

|+20| 380 |

884 – 400 = 484

Lesson 7: Share and critique strategies for varied addition and subtraction problems within 1,000.

Date: 10/23/13

5.A.76

Problem 3: 490 + 275

Have students solve this problem, then swap boards with their partner and follow these steps:

- Check to see if you got the same answer.
- Figure out and fix any mistakes.
- Study the strategy your partner used.
- Explain your partner's strategy. Take turns.
- Compare how your strategies are the same and how they are different.
- Decide which strategy is more efficient.
- Give your partner a compliment about her work. Be specific!

If time permits, repeat partner work following the suggested sequence: 380 + 223, 546 – 330, 811 – 692.

NOTES ON MULTIPLE MEANS OF REPRESENTATION:

Teach and post conversation starters to enhance the quality of pair-share conversations:

- I noticed that you….
- Your solution is different from / the same as mine because….
- I agree/disagree because….
- I like the way you….
- This strategy is more efficient, because….

Problem Set (10 minutes)

Students should do their personal best to complete the Problem Set within the allotted 10 minutes. For some classes, it may be appropriate to modify the assignment by specifying which problems they work on first. Some problems do not specify a method for solving. Students solve these problems using the RDW approach used for Application Problems.

Student Debrief (10 minutes)

Lesson Objective: Share and critique strategies for varied addition and subtraction problems within 1000.

The Student Debrief is intended to invite reflection and active processing of the total lesson experience.

Invite students to review their solutions for the Problem Set. They should check work by comparing answers with a partner before going over answers as a class. Look for misconceptions or misunderstandings that can be addressed in the Debrief. Guide students in a conversation to debrief the Problem Set and process the lesson.

You may choose to use any combination of the questions below to lead the discussion.

- For Problem 1, explain to your partner the mistake made in the second student work sample. Is compensation for addition the same

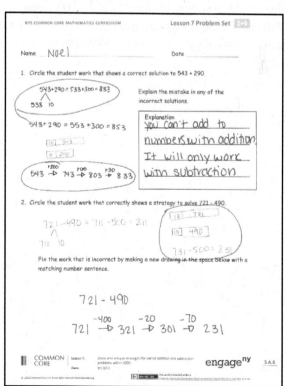

as for subtraction? Can you add the same amount to both addends without changing the total?

- In Problem 2, which student work sample incorrectly shows a strategy to solve 721 − 490? Share your new drawing and number sentence with a partner. How else could you have solved this problem?

- Which strategy do you prefer for solving Problem 3, the arrow way or a number bond? Why? What made the arrow way more challenging?

- What were you thinking when you selected a solution strategy to solve Problem 4? How was this similar to or different from your partner's strategy?

- What was the most important thing you learned today?

Exit Ticket (3 minutes)

After the Student Debrief, instruct students to complete the Exit Ticket. A review of their work will help you assess the students' understanding of the concepts that were presented in the lesson today and plan more effectively for future lessons. You may read the questions aloud to the students.

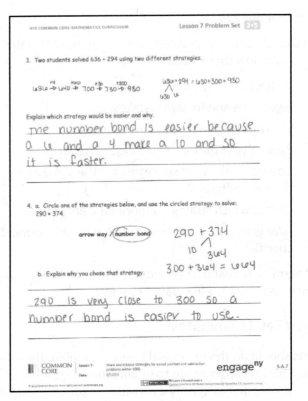

COMMON
CORE

Lesson 7: Share and critique strategies for varied addition and subtraction
problems within 1,000.

Date: 10/23/13

5.A.78

Name _____   Date _____

1. Circle the student work that shows a correct solution to 543 + 290.

543+290 = 533+300 = 833

533   10

Explain the mistake in any of the incorrect solutions.

543+290 = 553 +300 = 853

| 10 | 543 |

| 10 | 290 |

```
      +200        +60        +30
543 ─➤ 743 ─➤ 803 ─➤ 8 33
```

Explanation:
_____

_____

_____

_____

2. Circle the student work that correctly shows a strategy to solve 721 – 490.

721 –490 = 711 –500 = 211

711   10

| 10 | 721 |

| 10 | 490 |

731 –500 = 231

Fix the work that is incorrect by making a new drawing in the space below with a matching number sentence.

COMMON CORE

Lesson 7:   Share and critique strategies for varied addition and subtraction problems within 1,000.

Date: 10/23/13

5.A.79

3. Two students solved 636 + 294 using two different strategies.

$$636 \xrightarrow{+4} 640 \xrightarrow{+60} 700 \xrightarrow{+30} 730 \xrightarrow{+200} 930$$

$$636 + 294 = 630 + 300 = 930$$

630 6

Explain which strategy would be easier and why.

_____

_____

_____

_____

4. a. Circle one of the strategies below and use the circled strategy to solve
290 + 374.

arrow way / number bond

b. Explain why you chose that strategy.

_____

_____

_____

_____

COMMON CORE™ | Lesson 7:   Share and critique strategies for varied addition and subtraction problems within 1,000.

Date: 10/23/13   5.A.80

Name _____   Date _____

1. a. Circle one of the strategies below, and use the circled strategy to solve
        490 + 463.

    arrow way / number bond

    b. Explain why you chose that strategy.

    _____

    _____

    _____

    _____

 | Lesson 7:
| Date:

Share and critique strategies for varied addition and subtraction
problems within 1,000.
10/23/13

5.A.81

Name _____   Date _____

1. Solve each problem with a written strategy such as a tape diagram, a number bond, the arrow way, the vertical method, or chips on a place value chart.

a.	b.	c.
370 + 300 = _____	_____ = 562 – 200	_____ + 500 = 812

d.	e.	f.
230 - 190 = _____	_____ = 640 – 180	450 - 290 = _____

2. Use the arrow way to complete the number sentences.

a.	b.	c.
420 - 230 = _____	340 - 160 = _____	710 – 350 = _____

COMMON CORE™   Lesson 7:   Share and critique strategies for varied addition and subtraction problems within 1,000.   5.A.82

Date: 10/23/13

3. Solve 867 + 295 using two different strategies.

a.	b.

Tell which strategy you found easier to use when solving and explain why.

_____

_____

_____

_____

4. a. Circle one strategy to solve the problem 199 + 478.

arrow way / number bond

b. Solve using the strategy you circled.

COMMON CORE | Lesson 7: | Share and critique strategies for varied addition and subtraction problems within 1,000. | 5.A.83
| Date: | 10/23/13 |

© 2013 Common Core, Inc. All rights reserved. commoncore.org

Topic B

Strategies for Composing Tens and Hundreds Within 1,000

2.NBT.7, 2.NBT.9

Focus Standard:	2.NBT.7	Add and subtract within 1000, using concrete models or drawings and strategies based on place value, properties of operations, and/or the relationship between addition and subtraction; relate the strategy to a written method. Understand that in adding or subtracting three-digit numbers, one adds or subtracts hundreds and hundreds, tens and tens, ones and ones; and sometimes it is necessary to compose or decompose tens or hundreds.
	2.NBT.9	Explain why addition and subtraction strategies work, using place value and the properties of operations. (Explanations may be supported by drawings or objects.)
Instructional Days:	5	
Coherence -Links from:	G1–M6	Place Value, Comparison, Addition and Subtraction to 100
-Links to:	G3–M2	Place Value and Problem Solving with Units of Measure

Topic B in Module 5 is analogous to Topic B in Module 4, but while in Module 4 students composed ones and tens within 200, Module 5 expands upon this, finding students composing tens and hundreds within 1,000. The work of Topic A transitions naturally into Topic B, with students employing concrete and pictorial representations of the vertical algorithm when they encounter addition problems for which they do not have an obvious simplifying strategy.

In Lessons 8–9, students continue to build their conceptual understanding as they relate manipulatives to the algorithm, recording compositions as *new groups below* in vertical form as they did in Module 4. As they move the manipulatives, students use place value language to express the action and physically exchange 10 ones for 1 ten and 10 tens for 1 hundred, as needed. They record each change in the written vertical method, step by step.

In Lessons 10 and 11, students move from concrete conception to pictorial representation as they draw chip models to represent addition

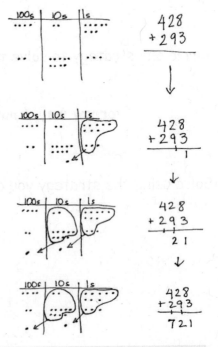

within 1,000. As they did with the manipulatives, students record each action in their drawings step by step on the algorithm (see image at right).

In Lesson 12, students are presented with a variety of problems for which they must choose an appropriate strategy to solve. Students are encouraged to be flexible in their thinking and to defend their reasoning using place value language. They may choose to represent and solve problems using number bonds, the arrow way, number disks, or chip models.

A Teaching Sequence Towards Mastery of Strategies for Composing Tens and Hundreds Within 1000

Objective 1: Relate manipulative representations to the addition algorithm.
(Lessons 8–9)

Objective 2: Use math drawings to represent additions with up to two compositions and relate drawings to the addition algorithm.
(Lessons 10–11)

Objective 3: Choose and explain solution strategies and record with a written addition method.
(Lesson 12)

Lesson 8

Objective: Relate manipulative representations to the addition algorithm.

Suggested Lesson Structure

■	Application Problem	(5 minutes)
■	Fluency Practice	(12 minutes)
■	Concept Development	(33 minutes)
■	Student Debrief	(10 minutes)
	Total Time	**(60 minutes)**

Application Problem (5 minutes)

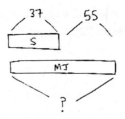

Susan has 37 pennies.

M.J. has 55 pennies more than Susan.

 a. How many pennies does M.J. have?

 b. How many pennies do they have altogether?

Note: Some students may read Part B and incorrectly add 37 + 55. Once the students have been given the opportunity to solve using any number of written strategies, invite some to share their representations of the problem.

Fluency Practice (12 minutes)

| ▪ Add Common Units **2.NBT.7** | (3 minutes) |
| ▪ Sprint: Two-Digit Addition **2.NBT.5** | (9 minutes) |

Add Common Units (3 minutes)

Materials: (S) Personal white boards

Note: Reviewing this mental math fluency will prepare students for understanding the importance of the written addition method.

 T: 2 puppies plus 1 puppy is…?

 S: 3 puppies.

 T: 3 dogs, 2 puppies, plus 1 puppy is…?

Lesson 8: Relate manipulative representations to the addition algorithm.
Date: 10/23/13

5.B.3

S: 3 dogs 3 puppies.

T: (Project 303.) Say the number in unit form.

S: 3 hundreds 3 ones.

T: (Write 303 + 202 = ____.) Say the addition sentence and answer in unit form.

S: 3 hundreds 3 ones + 2 hundreds 2 ones = 5 hundreds 5 ones.

T: Write the addition sentence on your personal boards.

S: (Write 303 + 202 = 505.)

Repeat this process for the following sequence: 404 + 203, 660 + 110, 707 + 220, 770 + 202, 440 + 340.

Sprint: Two-Digit Addition (9 minutes)

Materials: (S) Two-Digit Addition Sprint

Note: Students review two-digit addition in preparation for adding three-digit numbers in the lesson.

Concept Development (33 minutes)

Materials: (T) Place value disks, place value chart   (S) Personal white board, place value chart, place value disks (9 hundreds, 18 tens, 18 ones) per pair

T: What is 200 + 300?

S: 500.

T: Talk to your partner for 15 seconds about how you know.

S: I started at 300 and I counted on 2 more hundreds. → 2 + 3 = 5, so 2 hundreds + 3 hundreds is 5 hundreds.

T: What is 440 + 200?

S: 640.

T: Talk to your partner for 15 seconds about how you know.

S: I started at 440 and I counted on 2 hundreds so 440, 540, 640. → I know that 400 + 200 is 600, and then I just added on 40.

T: What is 287 + 314?

S: (Solve problem with partner or independently.)

S: 601.

T: Why was this problem more difficult to solve mentally?

S: We weren't just adding on another hundred. → It's easy to add on hundreds and tens. → This time we had to worry about the ones place, too.

T: What would be a better way to solve this problem to be sure we get the right answer?

S: Use number disks and place value charts. → Make a math drawing and show new units on the written addition.

T: Let's try a few more problems that might require the written addition.

Lesson 8:   Relate manipulative representations to the addition algorithm.

Date: 10/23/13

5.B.4

Note: In the following modeled activity, it is important to relate each action on the place value chart to the written vertical method for addition.

Problem 1: 303 + 37

T: (Write 303 + 37 on the board horizontally.) Read the problem aloud.

S: (Read 303 + 37 chorally.)

T: Talk with your partner. How could you solve this problem using mental math?

S: 303 + 30 + 7. → Add 3 and 7, which makes 10, then add 300 + 30 + 10. → 37 + 3 is 40, plus the 3 hundreds is 340.

T: Can we check our work using the written form?

S: Yes.

T: Let's try that.

T: Turn and talk: How do we set up this problem to record it vertically?

S: Write 303 on the top and 37 on the bottom. → Line up the ones and line up the tens.

T: (Rewrite the problem vertically.)

T: Let's solve using our number disks and place value charts.

T: How many hundreds do we need for the first addend, the first part?

S: 3 hundreds!

T: How many tens?

S: Zero!

T: How many ones?

S: 3 ones!

T: Count with me to set up the place value chart. (Point to chips on place value chart.)

S: (Count chorally.) 100, 200, 300, 301, 302, 303.

T: (Repeat the above process for the other part, 37.)

T: Does this model match the written vertical addition?

S: Yes!

T: Okay, we're ready to solve! (Point to the ones disks, then point to the ones in the written addition.) 3 ones + 7 ones is...?

S: 10 ones!

T: What do you see, and what should we do?

S: We made a ten! → Change 10 ones for 1 ten. → Remove 10 ones and put a ten-disk in the tens place because 10 ones is 1 ten. → We should compose a new unit, a ten!

T: That's right! We rename 10 ones as 1 ten. And where does the new unit of ten belong?

S: In the tens place!

T: Yes! (Model changing 10 ones for 1 ten.)

T: How do we record new groups below on our written addition? Turn and talk.

S: Write 1 ten below the tens column and 0 ones below the ones column. → Write 1 on the line under the 3 in the tens place, and write 0 under the line in the ones place.

T: Why do we write the one here? (Point to the line below the tens column.)

S: Because the 1 is actually a ten. → We made a ten so we put it in the tens column.

T: Now, let's add the tens. (Point to the tens disks.) 0 tens + 3 tens + 1 ten?

S: 4 tens!

T: Did we make a new hundred?

S: No!

T: (Model recording 4 tens in the tens place.)

T: Now, let's move on to the next larger unit, the hundreds. How many hundreds do we have?

S: 3 hundreds!

T: Turn and talk: Where do we record that on the written addition?

S: Write 3 in the hundreds place.

T: What is 303 + 37?

S: 340!

T: Explain to your partner how each change that I modeled on my place value chart matches each step that I recorded in the written addition.

S: 3 ones + 7 ones is 10 ones, so we renamed 10 ones for 1 ten and wrote the 1 on the line as new groups below. → There are 4 tens, so we wrote 4 below the line in the tens place.

Distribute place value charts and disks. Instruct students to work with a partner on the next problem.

Problem 2: 211 + 95

T: Now it's your turn. (Write 211 + 95 on the board vertically.) Write 211 + 95 as I did.

T: Turn and talk: How can we solve this mentally?

S: I take apart the numbers 200 + 10 + 1 + 90 + 5, and I get 200 + 100 + 6, which is 306. → 211 plus 9 tens is 301 plus 5 more is 306.

T: How can we check our mental math to be sure we are correct?

S: Use number disks. → Make a math drawing.

T: Model both addends on your place value chart.

> **NOTES ON MULTIPLE MEANS OF ACTION AND EXPRESSION:**
>
> For Problem 2, invite students to whisper count as partners take turns modeling and writing each addend. They may be encouraged to count the regular way (i.e., 10, 20, 30…) or the Say Ten way (i.e., 2 hundreds 1 ten 1, etc.). Partners also take turns recording their actions using the algorithm. This is an opportunity for the teacher to support struggling students in small group instruction.

T: We're ready to solve! Let's begin with the ones place. (Point to disks.) 1 one plus 5 ones?

S: 6 ones.

T: Use your disks to show what we should do here. (Circulate to check for understanding.)

T: Let's record the total number of ones on our written addition. (Write 6 in the ones place as students do the same.)

T: Let's move on to the tens place. (Point to disks.) What are you adding?

S: 1 ten and 9 tens.

T: How many tens do we have all together?

S: 10 tens!

T: What should we do?

MP.8

S: Bundle 10 tens and make a hundred. → Change 10 ten disks for 1 hundred disk. → Compose a new unit, a hundred!

S: (Make change on place value charts.)

T: Show your work in the written addition using new groups below. (Circulate as students record 1 on the line in the hundreds place and 0 in the tens place, in that order.)

T: Now, let's add the hundreds. How many hundreds?

S: 3 hundreds!

T: Yes! You remembered to add the new unit! So we write 3 below the line in the hundreds place.

T: Explain to your partner how your work with the disks matches the written addition and your number disks.

NOTES ON MULTIPLE MEANS OF ENGAGEMENT

Some students will struggle with precision and organization. Encourage them to visualize the ten-frame when arranging their disks into 5-groups. Also, help students line up their problems according to place value; instruct them to use lined paper turned 90 degrees (landscape orientation) and to write their numbers between the lines.

Continue with the following possible sequence: 324 + 156, 546 + 273, 435 + 382. As students demonstrate confidence in relating their models to the written addition, allow them to work independently on the Problem Set.

Problem Set (10 minutes)

Students should do their personal best to complete the Problem Set within the allotted 10 minutes. For some classes, it may be appropriate to modify the assignment by specifying which problems they work on first. Some problems do not specify a method for solving. Students solve these problems using the RDW approach used for Application Problems.

Student Debrief (10 minutes)

Lesson Objective: Relate manipulative representations to the addition algorithm.

The Student Debrief is intended to invite reflection and active processing of the total lesson experience.

Invite students to review their solutions for the Problem Set. They should check work by comparing answers with a partner before going over answers as a class. Look for misconceptions or misunderstandings that can be addressed in the Debrief. Guide students in a conversation to debrief the Problem Set and process the lesson.

You may choose to use any combination of the questions below to lead the discussion.

- How did you solve Problem 1(a), 301 + 49, 402 + 48? Did you begin by adding the ones only? Why didn't you need to solve with number disks? How can you check your mental math? Where did you write the new unit?

- Explain to your partner how you used manipulatives to solve Problem 1(b). Did you need to bundle a new ten or hundred? How did you know? How did you show it using the algorithm?

- For Problem 1(c), how did your work with the number disks match the written addition? How did you show new groups below? How were these problems different from the ones in Problem 1(b)?

- What do you notice about the answers for Problem 1(d)? If the addends in each problem are different, why are the answers the same? For Problem 2, which problems did you solve using number disks and a place value chart? How do you know when you should solve using a place value chart, a simplifying strategy, or mental math?

- Did you notice any patterns in Problem 2 that helped you to solve efficiently? Did you use a place value chart every time you composed a new unit of ten or a hundred?

NYS COMMON CORE MATHEMATICS CURRICULUM   Lesson 8 Problem Set

Name Noel   Date

1. Solve the following problems using any method. Check your work with the vertical method and number disks.

a. 301 + 49

```
   301
 +  49
 ─────
   350
```

402 + 48

```
   402
 +  48
 ─────
   450
```

b. 315 + 93

```
   315
 +  93
 ─────
   408
```

216 + 192

```
   216
 + 192
 ─────
   408
```

c. 545 + 346

```
   545
 + 346
 ─────
   891
```

565 + 226

```
   565
 + 226
 ─────
   791
```

d. 222 + 687

```
   687
 + 222
 ─────
   909
```

164 + 745

```
   745
 + 164
 ─────
   909
```

COMMON CORE   Lesson 8:   Relate manipulative representations to the addition algorithm.   engage^ny   5.B.9

NYS COMMON CORE MATHEMATICS CURRICULUM   Lesson 8 Problem Set

2. Solve using mental math or your number disks.

a. 300 + 200   500

b. 320 + 200   520

c. 320 + 230   550

d. 320 + 280   600

e. 328 + 286   614

f. 600 + 80   680

g. 600 + 180   780

h. 620 + 180   800

i. 680 + 220   900

j. 680 + 230   910

COMMON CORE   Lesson 8:   Relate manipulative representations to the addition algorithm.   engage^ny   5.B.10

COMMON CORE | Lesson 8:   Relate manipulative representations to the addition algorithm.
                  | Date: 10/23/13

5.B.8

Exit Ticket (3 minutes)

After the Student Debrief, instruct students to complete the Exit Ticket. A review of their work will help you assess the students' understanding of the concepts that were presented in the lesson today and plan more effectively for future lessons. You may read the questions aloud to the students.

Lesson 8:   Relate manipulative representations to the addition algorithm.
Date: 10/23/13

5.B.9

A

Add.

Correct _____

1	38 + 1 =		23	85 + 7 =	
2	47 + 2 =		24	85 + 9 =	
3	56 + 3 =		25	76 + 4 -	
4	65 + 4 =		26	76 + 5 =	
5	31 + 8 =		27	76 + 6 =	
6	42 + 7 =		28	76 + 9 =	
7	53 + 6 =		29	64 + 6 =	
8	64 + 5 =		30	64 + 7 =	
9	49 + 1 =		31	76 + 8 =	
10	49 + 2 =		32	43 + 7 =	
11	49 + 3 =		33	43 + 8 =	
12	49 + 5 =		34	43 + 9 =	
13	58 + 2 =		35	52 + 8 =	
14	58 + 3 =		36	52 + 9 =	
15	58 + 4 =		37	59 + 1 =	
16	58 + 6 =		38	59 + 3 =	
17	67 + 3 =		39	58 + 2 =	
18	57 + 4 =		40	58 + 4 =	
19	57 + 5 =		41	77 + 3 =	
20	57 + 7 =		42	77 + 5 =	
21	85 + 5 =		43	35 + 5 =	
22	85 + 6 =		44	35 + 8 =	

© Bill Davidson

COMMON CORE | Lesson 8: | Relate manipulative representations to the addition algorithm.
| Date: | 10/23/13

5.B.10

B

Improvement _____   # Correct _____

Add.

1	28 + 1 =		23	75 + 7 =	
2	37 + 2 =		24	75 + 9 =	
3	46 + 3 =		25	66 + 4 =	
4	55 + 4 =		26	66 + 5 =	
5	21 + 8 =		27	66 + 6 =	
6	32 + 7 =		28	66 + 9 =	
7	43 + 6 =		29	54 + 6 =	
8	54 + 5 =		30	54 + 7 =	
9	39 + 1 =		31	54 + 8 =	
10	39 + 2 =		32	33 + 7 =	
11	39 + 3 =		33	33 + 8 =	
12	39 + 5 =		34	33 + 9 =	
13	48 + 2 =		35	42 + 8 =	
14	48 + 3 =		36	42 + 9 =	
15	48 + 4 =		37	49 + 1 =	
16	48 + 6 =		38	49 + 3 =	
17	57 + 3 =		39	58 + 2 =	
18	57 + 4 =		40	58 + 4 =	
19	57 + 5 =		41	67 + 3 =	
20	57 + 7 =		42	67 + 5 =	
21	75 + 5 =		43	85 + 5 =	
22	75 + 6 =		44	85 + 8 =	

© Bill Davidson

Lesson 8:   Relate manipulative representations to the addition algorithm.
Date: 10/23/13

5.B.11

Name _____   Date _____

1. Solve the following problems using any method. Check your work with the vertical method and number disks.

   a. 301 + 49   402 + 48

   b. 315 + 93   216 + 192

   c. 545 + 346   565 + 226

   d. 222 + 687   164 + 745

2. Solve using mental math or your number disks.

   a. 300 + 200

   b. 320 + 200

   c. 320 + 230

   d. 320 + 280

   e. 328 + 286

   f. 600 + 80

   g. 600 + 180

   h. 620 + 180

   i. 680 + 220

   j. 680 + 230

Name _____   Date _____

1. Solve the following problems using the vertical method, your place value chart, and number disks. Bundle a ten or hundred when necessary.

   a. 378 + 113

   b. 178 + 141

Name _____   Date _____

1. Solve the following problems using the vertical method, your place value chart, and number disks. Bundle a ten or hundred when necessary.

   a. 505 + 75   606 + 84

   b. 293 + 114   314 + 495

   c. 364 + 326   346 + 234

   d. 384 + 225   609 + 351

Date: 10/23/13

2. Solve using mental math or your number disks.

   a. 200 + 400

   b. 220 + 400

   c. 220 + 440

   d. 220 + 480

   e. 225 + 485

   f. 500 + 60

   g. 500 + 160

   h. 540 + 160

   i. 560 + 240

   j. 560 + 250

COMMON CORE™ | Lesson 8: Relate manipulative representations to the addition algorithm.
Date: 10/23/13

5.B.16

Lesson 9

Objective: Relate manipulative representations to the addition algorithm.

Suggested Lesson Structure

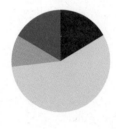

■ Fluency Practice	(10 minutes)
■ Application Problem	(6 minutes)
▢ Concept Development	(34 minutes)
■ Student Debrief	(10 minutes)
Total Time	**(60 minutes)**

Application Problem (6 minutes)

The table to the right represents the halftime score at a basketball game.

The red team scored 19 points in the second half.

The yellow team scored 13 points in the second half.

    a.   Who won the game?

    b.   By how much did that team win?

Red Team	63 points
Yellow Team	71 points

Note: This comparison problem requires multiple steps. The numbers chosen encourage students to practice simplifying and place value strategies. Invite students to reason about how they could have known who won without adding.

Fluency Practice (10 minutes)

- Making the Next Ten to Add   **2.OA.2, 2.NBT.5**   (2 minutes)
- Add Common Units   **2.NBT.1, 2.NBT.7**   (2 minutes)
- More Tens and Ones   **2.NBT.5, 2.NBT.7**   (6 minutes)

Making the Next Ten to Add (2 minutes)

Note: This fluency will review foundations that will lead into today's lesson.

    T: When I say, 9 + 4, you say 10 + 3. Ready? 9 + 4.

    S: 10 + 3.

    T: Answer.

    S: 13.

Post on board:
9 + 4 = _____
∧
1   3

Continue with the following possible sequence: 19 + 4, 9 + 6, 19 + 6, 8 + 3, 18 + 3, 8 + 5, 18 + 5, 7 + 6, 27 + 6, 7 + 4, 17 + 4, 9 + 7, 19 + 7, 8 + 6, 18 + 6.

Add Common Units (2 minutes)

Materials: (S) Personal white boards

Note: Reviewing this mental math fluency will prepare students for understanding the importance of the algorithm.

T: (Project 545.) Say the number in unit form.
S: 5 hundreds 4 tens 5 ones.
T: (Write 545 + 232 =____.) Say the addition sentence and answer in unit form.
S: 5 hundreds 4 tens 5 ones + 2 hundreds 3 tens 2 ones = 7 hundreds 7 tens 7 ones.
T: Write the addition sentence on your personal boards.
S: (Write 454 + 232 = 777.)

Repeat the process and continue with the following possible sequence: 440 + 225, 603 + 303, 211 + 644, 770 + 330, 771 + 341.

More Tens and Ones (6 minutes)

Note: Students review adding tens and ones to prepare for the lesson.

T: What is 3 tens more than 6 tens?
S: 9 tens.
T: Give the number sentence in unit form.
S: 6 tens + 3 tens = 9 tens.
T: Give the number sentence in standard form.
S: 60 + 30 = 90.
T: What is 4 tens more than 6 tens? Give the answer in tens.
S: 10 tens.
T: Give the answer in hundreds.
S: 1 hundred.
T: Give the number sentence in standard form.
S: 60 + 40 = 100.

Continue with the following possible sequence: 4 tens more than 6 tens 3 ones, 5 tens more than 5 tens, 5 tens more than 6 tens, 5 tens more than 6 tens 4 ones, 2 tens more than 8 tens, 3 tens more than 8 tens.

COMMON CORE

Lesson 9: Relate manipulative representations to the addition algorithm.
Date: 10/23/13

5.B.18

Concept Development (34 minutes)

Materials: (T) Place value disks (9 hundreds, 18 tens, 18 ones), personal white board (S) Place value disks (9 hundreds, 18 tens, 18 ones), personal white boards

Note: This lesson is designed to provide students with practice time for relating manipulative representations to written method. As students show proficiency, allow them to move on to the Problem Set. The first problem is intended for guided practice; the second problem is still guided but with less teacher support. Adjust delivery of instruction as best to fit student needs.

Problem 1: 427 + 385

Distribute number disks. Students can use their desks to model the problems below, perhaps by dividing their desks into three columns with masking tape.

NOTES ON MULTIPLE MEANS OF REPRESENTATION:

For accelerated learners, incorporate error analysis into the lesson. Distribute a pre-made, half-page extension with an incorrect problem (e.g., 679 + 284 = 863). Tell students that this is the Math ER! They must put on their doctor's jackets and diagnose the sick problem. On each slip of paper, ask two questions:

- What makes this problem sick?
- What steps should the doctor take to cure the problem?

T: (Write 427 + 385 in the vertical written form on the board. Next to the problem draw a number bond showing two parts: 427 and 385.)

T: Let's solve this mentally. Where do we begin?

S: Add the hundreds (400 + 300 = 700), then add the tens (20 + 80 = 100), then add the ones (7 + 5 = 12). Then add them together. 700 + 100 + 12 = 812. → Break the second part into hundreds, tens, and ones. 427 + 300 = 727 then, 727 + 80 = 807 and 807 + 5 = 812.

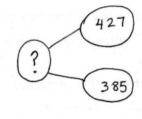

T: That might not be the easiest way for all of us. Is there another way we can solve?

S: Use number disks. → Make a math drawing. → Solve with the written addition.

T: Use place value language to tell your partner how to show this problem using number disks.

S: Show 4 hundred disks, 2 ten disks, and 7 one disks, then show 3 hundred disks, 8 tens, and 5 ones. → Show both parts so you can add them together. → Make sure you put the disks in the right part of your chart, like 7 ones and 5 ones go in the ones column to match the written problem.

T: Let's all show the problem. (Model counting out number disks as students do the same.)

T: What should we do first to solve?

S: Add the ones.

T: 7 ones + 5 ones?

S: 12 ones!

T: What do we do when we have 10 of a unit, like 10 ones?

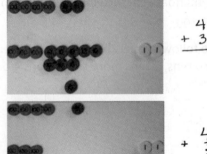

   Lesson 9:   Relate manipulative representations to the addition algorithm.
Date: 10/23/13

5.B.19

S: Change 10 ones for 1 ten. → Take off the 10 ones disks and put 1 ten disk. → Rename the 10 ones as a new unit of ten.

T: Yes! Let's do that together. (Model changing 10 ones for 1 ten.) Don't forget to show your action in the algorithm. (Circulate as students show the change on the written form using new groups below.)

S: (Write the ones digit first, since they are writing the number 12.)

T: What do we do next?

S: Add the tens. → Add 2 tens + 8 tens + 1 ten. → Add the tens, but don't forget the new ten that we wrote on the line.

T: Let's add 2 tens, 8 tens, and 1 ten. How many tens altogether?

S: 11 tens.

T: What's next?

S: Bundle to make a new unit, a hundred! → Change 10 tens for 1 hundred. → Take away the 10 tens disks and put a hundred disk.

T: Yes, let's compose a new hundred! Remember to show the change using the addition algorithm. (Change 10 tens for 1 hundred and show the change using new groups below as students do the same.)

T: Are we ready to add the hundreds?

S: Yes!

T: What is 4 hundreds + 3 hundreds + 1 hundred?

S: 8 hundreds!

T: Let's record that. (Write 8 in the hundreds place as students do the same.) If 427 and 385 are the parts, what is the whole?

S: 812!

NOTES ON MULTIPLE MEANS OF ENGAGEMENT:

As students move towards independent practice, highlight critical vocabulary so they can ask themselves questions as they solve:

- Do I have enough *ones* or *tens* to *bundle*? (More abstractly we can ask, "Can I *compose* a new *unit*?")
- Where do I record the new *ten* or *hundred*?
- How do we show this change using the *algorithm*?

These questions will prepare students to work independently through the Problem Set and to meaningfully contribute during the Debrief.

Problem 2: 672 + 249

T: Write 672 + 249 vertically, and whisper-count as you show it on your place value chart. (Circulate as students count out place value disks and write the problem vertically.)

T: Are we finding a part or the whole?

S: The whole.

T: What are the parts?

S: 672 and 249.

T: (Draw a number bond on the board to show the two parts and the missing whole.)

T: Can we solve this mentally?

S: 600 + 200 + 70 + 40 + 2 + 9 equals 800 + 110 + 11 which equals 921. → 672 plus 200 is 872, plus 40 is 912, plus 9 more is 921.

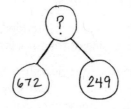

Lesson 9:   Relate manipulative representations to the addition algorithm.
Date: 10/23/13

5.B.20

T: That might not be the easiest way for all of us. Let's try that with the written addition and number disks.

T: What is the first step?

S: Add the ones. → Add 2 ones + 9 ones, which is 11 ones.

T: What do you do next? Discuss with your partner.

S: Make a ten! → Change 10 ones for 1 ten and record it in new groups below. → Compose a ten, and then you'll have one leftover.

T: Okay, show me with your disks and record it on the written addition. (Circulate as students work and check for understanding.)

T: Turn and talk, what is our next step?

S: Move on to the tens. → Add the tens, and don't forget the new one! → Add 7 tens + 4 tens + 1 ten.

T: You've got it! Show me and record it! (Circulate and check for understanding.)

T: What is our next step?

S: Add the hundreds. → Add 6 hundreds + 2 hundreds + 1 hundred.

T: One last time, show me and record it! (Circulate and check for understanding.)

T: So, what is 672 + 249?

S: 921!

If students show proficiency after the two problems above, allow them to move on to the Problem Set. Otherwise, continue with the following suggested sequence: 671 + 149, 348 + 464, 563 + 247.

Problem Set (10 minutes)

Students should do their personal best to complete the Problem Set within the allotted 10 minutes. For some classes, it may be appropriate to modify the assignment by specifying which problems they work on first. Some problems do not specify a method for solving. Students solve these problems using the RDW approach used for Application Problems.

Student Debrief (10 minutes)

Lesson Objective: Relate manipulative representations to the addition algorithm.

The Student Debrief is intended to invite reflection and active processing of the total lesson experience.

Invite students to review their solutions for the Problem Set. They should check work by comparing answers with a partner before going over answers as a class. Look for misconceptions or misunderstandings that can be addressed in the Debrief. Guide students in a

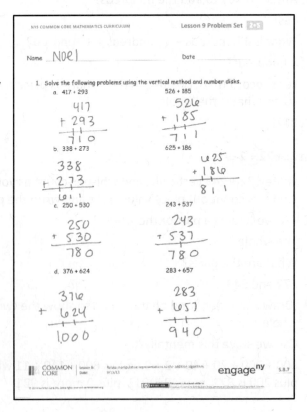

conversation to debrief the Problem Set and process the lesson.

You may choose to use any combination of the questions below to lead the discussion.

- Did you solve any problems on the first page mentally or with a simplifying strategy? Which ones? Explain your thinking.

- Explain to your partner how you used manipulatives to set up the problems in 1(a). How did you change your number disks to show the problem in the second column? What actions did you take to solve?

- For Problem 1(b), how did your work with the number disks match the written addition? How did you show new groups below?

- Explain to your partner how you solved Problem 1(c). Did you need to compose a ten or hundred for the second problem in the set? Why not? Why was the total the same for both problems?

- In Problem 2, which problems were you able to solve mentally? Did you use manipulatives to solve any of these problems? Why or why not

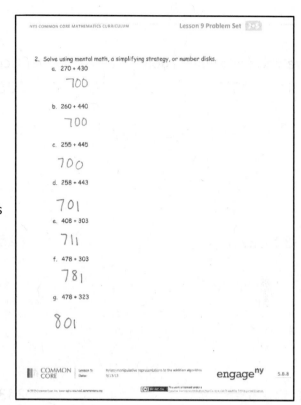

- Use place value language and explain to your partner how you solved Problem 2(a–d) mentally. Or explain how your place value chart and the written addition changed as you worked through the problems.

Exit Ticket (3 minutes)

After the Student Debrief, instruct students to complete the Exit Ticket. A review of their work will help you assess the students' understanding of the concepts that were presented in the lesson today and plan more effectively for future lessons. You may read the questions aloud to the students.

COMMON CORE™

Lesson 9:   Relate manipulative representations to the addition algorithm.
Date: 10/23/13

5.B.22

Name _____ Date _____

1. Solve the following problems using the vertical method and number disks.

   a. 417 + 293   526 + 185

   b. 338 + 273   625 + 186

   c. 250 + 530   243 + 537

   d. 376 + 624   283 + 657

2. Solve using mental math, a simplifying strategy, or number disks.

   a. 270 + 430

   b. 260 + 440

   c. 255 + 445

   d. 258 + 443

   e. 408 + 303

   f. 478 + 303

   g. 478 + 323

Lesson 9: Relate manipulative representations to the addition algorithm.
Date: 10/23/13

5.B.24

Name _____   Date _____

Solve the following problems using the vertical method, your place value chart, and number disks. Bundle a ten or hundred when necessary.

1. 375 + 197

2. 184 + 338

Name _____   Date _____

1. Solve the following problems using the vertical method, your place value chart and number disks. Bundle a ten or hundred when necessary.

   a. 205 + 345   365 + 406

   b. 446 + 334   466 + 226

   c. 537 + 243   358 + 443

   d. 753 + 157   663 + 258

COMMON CORE™   Lesson 9:   Relate manipulative representations to the addition algorithm.
                    Date: 10/23/13   5.B.26

© 2013 Common Core, Inc. All rights reserved. **commoncore.org**

2. Solve using mental math or number disks.

   a. 180 + 420

   b. 190 + 430

   c. 364 + 236

   d. 275 + 435

   e. 404 + 206

   f. 440 + 260

   g. 444 + 266

COMMON CORE | Lesson 9:   Relate manipulative representations to the addition algorithm.
  Date: 10/23/13

5.B.27

Lesson 10

Objective: Use math drawings to represent additions with up to two compositions and relate drawings to the addition algorithm.

Suggested Lesson Structure

■ Application Problem   (6 minutes)
■ Fluency Practice   (13 minutes)
■ Concept Development   (31 minutes)
■ Student Debrief   (10 minutes)

Total Time   **(60 minutes)**

Application Problem (6 minutes)

Benjie has 36 crayons. Ana has 12 fewer crayons than Benjie.

   a. How many crayons does Ana have?
   b. How many crayons do they have altogether?

Note: This problem is intended for guided practice to help students gain familiarity with the *compare with smaller unknown* problem type. The numbers are intentionally small to allow students to focus on the relationship between the numbers.

B [36   ]   36 – 12 = □

A [? | 12]   12 + □ = 36
      fewer
                      Ana has 24 crayons.

36 + 24 = □
    ⤬
  50   10
      They have 60 crayons
      altogether.

Fluency Practice (13 minutes)

▪ Compensation **2.NBT.5**   (4 minutes)
▪ Sprint: Addition Crossing Tens **2.OA.2, 2.NBT.5**   (9 minutes)

Compensation (4 minutes)

Note: This fluency drill reviews the mental math strategy of compensation. By making a multiple of 10, students solve a much simpler addition problem. Draw a number bond for the first problem on the board to help students visualize the decomposition.

   T: (Write 42 + 19 = _____.) Let's use a mental math strategy to add. How much more does 19 need to make the next ten?

42 + 19
  / \
41   1

41 + 20 = 61

Lesson 10:   Use math drawings to represent additions with up to two
             compositions and relate drawings to the addition algorithm.
Date: 10/23/13

5.B.28

S: 1 more.

T: Where can 19 get 1 more from?

S: From the 42!

T: Take 1 from 42 and give it to 19. Say the new number sentence with the answer.

S: 41 + 20 = 61.

T: 37 + 19.

S: 36 + 20 = 56.

Continue with the following possible sequence: 29 + 23, 38 + 19, 32 + 19, 24 + 17, 34 + 19.

Sprint: Addition Crossing Tens (9 minutes)

Materials: (S) Addition Crossing Tens Sprint

Note: This Sprint builds fluency with adding when crossing the next ten using mental strategies.

Concept Development (31 minutes)

Materials: (S) Math journals or paper

As students learn to make math drawings like the chip model to represent the written vertical method, it is important to emphasize precision in aligning digits in their proper place, drawing number disks in clear 5-groups, and showing new groups below in the correct place.

Problem 1: 126 + 160

T: (Write 126 + 160 vertically. Draw two long vertical lines, which serve as the place value chart, next to the written addition. See image at right.)

T: Let's show one part. How many hundreds in 126?

S: 1 hundred.

T: (Draw 1 hundred.) How many tens?

MP.6

S: 2 tens. (Count tens as the teacher draws.)

T: How many ones?

S: 6 ones. (Count ones as the teacher draws.)

T: Let's count the first part to be sure our model is correct.

S: 100, 110, 120, 121, 122, 123, 124, 125, 126.

T: Now, let's show the other part. (Repeat the process to model 160.)

> NOTES ON
> MULTIPLE MEANS OF
> ACTION AND
> EXPRESSION:
>
> Since it is important to teach precision when drawing chips and aligning digits, students should use a pencil and paper, which allows for greater accuracy than a white board marker. As they work through each problem step-by-step, students can highlight each column on the place value chart and on the written addition. Also, if a student continues to struggle with place value understanding, the teacher may wish to highlight the ones, tens, and hundreds columns in different colors.

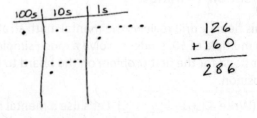

Lesson 10:	Use math drawings to represent additions with up to two compositions and relate drawings to the addition algorithm.
Date:	10/23/13

5.B.29

T:　Let's count the second part to check our model.

S:　100, 110, 120, 130, 140, 150, 160.

T:　It's important that our model matches the problem we're solving.

T:　Now, let's solve the problem. 6 ones + 0 ones?

S:　6 ones!

T:　Do we make a new ten?

S:　No!

T:　So we write the number of ones, 6, below the line in the ones place.

MP.6

T:　2 tens + 6 tens?

S:　8 tens!

T:　Do we make a new hundred?

S:　No!

T:　So we write the number of tens, 8, below the line in the tens place.

T:　1 hundred + 1 hundred?

S:　2 hundreds!

T:　We write the number of hundreds, 2, below the line in the hundreds place. Read the problem with me.

S:　126 + 160 = 286.

T:　Did we need to bundle units in this problem? Why or why not? Discuss with your partner.

S:　6 + 0 and 2 + 6 don't equal 10, and you only bundle when there are partners to ten or more. → The ones didn't make a ten and the tens didn't make a hundred. → First, I looked in the ones column, and 6 plus 0 doesn't make a new ten. Then, I looked in the tens column, and 20 plus 60 isn't enough to make a new hundred.

T:　Now, explain to your partner how the drawing matches the written addition. Explain your thinking using place value language.

Problem 2: 326 + 167

T:　Let's work through another problem together in your math journal. Turn your journal so the lines are already vertical on the page for easy setup. (Repeat the above process to model 326 + 167.)

T:　Let's begin by adding the ones. Look at the written addition and the model. Tell your partner what you notice. How are they the same?

S:　They both show 6 and 7. → They show the same parts. → They both show 13 ones, but one is dots and the other is numbers.

T:　Aha! They show the same total and that total is 13! What do we do now?

S:　Bundle 10 ones as 1 ten! → Compose a ten! → Rename 13 ones as 1 ten 3 ones!

T:　Excellent! Remember, what we do on the model, we do to the numbers. We composed a ten, so we circle the 10 ones and draw an arrow into the tens place, where we draw the new unit of 10. (See image at right.)

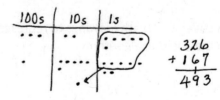

T: Using the algorithm, we show this new unit of 10 by writing a 1 on the line below the tens place. This way we remember to add it in when we count the tens.

T: We write 3 below the line in the ones place. When we look at the model, we see there are 3 dots left.

T: Now let's add the tens. Remember to add the new unit. (Point to the model.) 2 tens + 6 tens + 1 ten is...?

S: 9 tens!

T: Did we make a new hundred?

S: No!

T: So we write 9 tens below the line in the tens place.

T: And now let's add our hundreds. 3 hundreds + 1 hundred is...?

S: 4 hundreds!

T: We record the digit 4 below the line in the hundreds place. Read the entire problem.

S: 326 + 167 = 493.

T: How does each step in the drawing match what we do in the written addition? Talk with your partner. Explain your thinking using place value language.

T: Now, it's your turn. Draw a model and use it to solve 462 + 284. I'll walk around to see how it's going.

> **NOTES ON MULTIPLE MEANS OF ENGAGEMENT:**
>
> Use a simple rhythm or jingle to help students remember the key concept of composing a new unit. For example:
>
> - "Add your ones up first! Make a bundle if you can!"
> - "Add your tens up next! Make a bundle if you can!"

Follow the above procedure to guide students as they write 462 + 284 vertically, model it, and solve. Remind students to be precise in lining up the digits and in drawing their number disks in neat 5-groups. Have them use place value language to explain each action they take on their model and how it is represented in the written addition.

Repeat the process for 487 + 345 with two renamings. Continue to support struggling students, but as students demonstrate proficiency, instruct them to work on the Problem Set independently.

Problem Set (10 minutes)

Students should do their personal best to complete the Problem Set within the allotted 10 minutes. For some classes, it may be appropriate to modify the assignment by specifying which problems they work on first. Some problems do not specify a method for solving. Students solve these problems using the RDW approach used for Application Problems.

Student Debrief (10 minutes)

Lesson Objective: Use math drawings to represent additions with up to two compositions and relate drawings to the addition algorithm.

Lesson 10:   Use math drawings to represent additions with up to two compositions and relate drawings to the addition algorithm.

Date: 10/23/13

5.B.31

The Student Debrief is intended to invite reflection and active processing of the total lesson experience.

Invite students to review their solutions for the Problem Set. They should check work by comparing answers with a partner before going over answers as a class. Look for misconceptions or misunderstandings that can be addressed in the Debrief. Guide students in a conversation to debrief the Problem Set and process the lesson.

You may choose to use any combination of the questions below to lead the discussion.

- Explain to your partner how you solved Problem 1(a) using the chip model and the written method. How could you solve this problem differently using a simplifying strategy?

- For Problem 1(b), how did you know whether or not to bundle a new unit of 10 or 100?

- For Problem 1(c), where did you write the new ten or hundred in the written addition? How did the algorithm match your chip model? How was this different from Problem 1(b)?

- What was interesting about Problem 1(d)? Could you have solved this problem mentally using your understanding of place value?

- Jade uses place value language to argue that the answer to Problem 2(a), 546 + 162, is 6 hundreds, 10 tens, 8 ones. Sam says that it is 7 hundreds, 8 ones. Who is correct? How do you know?

- How did you solve Problem 2(a)? How did you change your place value chart to show Problem 2(b)? Did you compose a new unit of 10 or 100 in both problems?

Exit Ticket (3 minutes)

After the Student Debrief, instruct students to complete the Exit Ticket. A review of their work will help you assess the students' understanding of the concepts that were presented in the lesson today and plan more effectively for future lessons. You may read the questions aloud to the students.

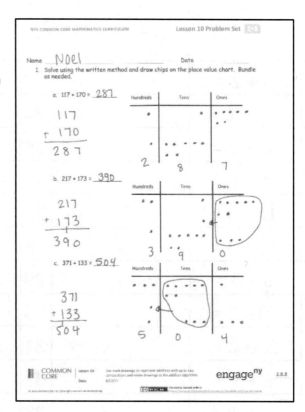

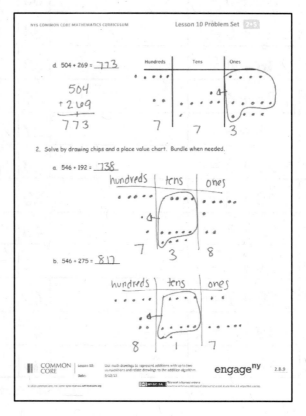

Lesson 10:   Use math drawings to represent additions with up to two
compositions and relate drawings to the addition algorithm.

Date: 10/23/13

5.B.32

A

Correct _____

Add.

1	8 + 2 =		23	18 + 6 =	
2	18 + 2 =		24	28 + 6 =	
3	38 + 2 =		25	16 + 8 =	
4	7 + 3 =		26	26 + 8 =	
5	17 + 3 =		27	18 + 7 =	
6	37 + 3 =		28	18 + 8 =	
7	8 + 3 =		29	28 + 7 =	
8	18 + 3 =		30	28 + 8 =	
9	28 + 3 =		31	15 + 9 =	
10	6 + 5 =		32	16 + 9 =	
11	16 + 5 =		33	25 + 9 =	
12	26 + 5 =		34	26 + 9 =	
13	18 + 4 =		35	14 + 7 =	
14	28 + 4 =		36	16 + 6 =	
15	16 + 6 =		37	15 + 8 =	
16	26 + 6 =		38	23 + 8 =	
17	18 + 5 =		39	25 + 7 =	
18	28 + 5 =		40	15 + 7 =	
19	16 + 7 =		41	24 + 7 =	
20	26 + 7 =		42	14 + 9 =	
21	19 + 2 =		43	19 + 8 =	
22	17 + 4 =		44	28 + 9 =	

© Bill Davidson

COMMON CORE

Lesson 10: Use math drawings to represent additions with up to two compositions and relate drawings to the addition algorithm.

Date: 10/23/13

5.B.33

B

Improvement _____   # Correct _____

Add.

1	9 + 1 =		23	19 + 5 =	
2	19 + 1 =		24	29 + 5 =	
3	39 + 1 =		25	17 + 7 =	
4	6 + 4 =		26	27 + 7 =	
5	16 + 4 =		27	19 + 6 =	
6	36 + 4 =		28	19 + 7 =	
7	9 + 2 =		29	29 + 6 =	
8	19 + 2 =		30	29 + 7 =	
9	29 + 2 =		31	17 + 8 =	
10	7 + 4 =		32	17 + 9 =	
11	17 + 4 =		33	27 + 8 =	
12	27 + 4 =		34	27 + 9 =	
13	19 + 3 =		35	12 + 9 =	
14	29 + 3 =		36	14 + 8 =	
15	17 + 5 =		37	16 + 7 =	
16	27 + 5 =		38	28 + 6 =	
17	19 + 4 =		39	26 + 8 =	
18	29 + 4 =		40	24 + 8 =	
19	17 + 6 =		41	13 + 8 =	
20	27 + 6 =		42	24 + 9 =	
21	18 + 3 =		43	29 + 8 =	
22	26 + 5 =		44	18 + 9 =	

© Bill Davidson

COMMON CORE™   Lesson 10:   Use math drawings to represent additions with up to two compositions and relate drawings to the addition algorithm.

Date: 10/23/13

5.B.34

Name _____   Date _____

1. Solve using the written method and draw chips on the place value chart. Bundle as needed.

Hundreds	Tens	Ones

117 + 170 = _____

Hundreds	Tens	Ones

217 + 173 = _____

Hundreds	Tens	Ones

371 + 133 = _____

COMMON CORE

Lesson 10:   Use math drawings to represent additions with up to two
            compositions and relate drawings to the addition algorithm.
Date: 10/23/13

5.B.35

Hundreds	Tens	Ones

504 + 269 = _____

2. Solve by drawing chips and a place value chart. Bundle when needed.

a. 546 + 192 = _____

b. 546 + 275 = _____

COMMON CORE™   **Lesson 10:**   Use math drawings to represent additions with up to two
                              compositions and relate drawings to the addition algorithm.   5.B.36
                   Date: 10/23/13

Name _____   Date _____

Solve by drawing chips on a place value chart. Bundle as needed.

1. 436 + 509 = _____

2. 584 + 361 = _____

Lesson 10: Use math drawings to represent additions with up to two
           compositions and relate drawings to the addition algorithm.

Date: 10/23/13

5.B.37

Name _____   Date _____

1. Solve using the written method and draw chips on the place value chart. Bundle as needed.

Hundreds	Tens	Ones

124 + 260 = _____

Hundreds	Tens	Ones

426 + 324 = _____

Hundreds	Tens	Ones

362 + 243 = _____

COMMON CORE™

Lesson 10: Use math drawings to represent additions with up to two compositions and relate drawings to the addition algorithm.

Date: 10/23/13

5.B.38

Hundreds	Tens	Ones

606 + 294 = _____

2. Solve by drawing chips and a place value chart. Bundle when needed.

a. 372 + 118 = _____

b. 248 + 233 = _____

COMMON CORE™

Lesson 10: Use math drawings to represent additions with up to two
compositions and relate drawings to the addition algorithm.

Date: 10/23/13

5.B.39

Lesson 11

Objective: Use math drawings to represent additions with up to two compositions and relate drawings to the addition algorithm.

Suggested Lesson Structure

- Application Problem   (5 minutes)
- Fluency Practice   (10 minutes)
- Concept Development   (35 minutes)
- Student Debrief   (10 minutes)

  Total Time   **(60 minutes)**

**NOTES ON
MULTIPLE MEANS OF
REPRESENTATION:**

Since we do not expect students to work the algorithm without place value charts and manipulatives in Grade 2, allow students to use disks to calculate the solution and to explain their thinking. They can even use straws to represent the pencils in the Application Problem.

Application Problem (5 minutes)

Mr. Arnold has a box of pencils. He passes out 27 pencils and has 45 left. How many pencils did Mr. Arnold have in the beginning?

Note: This is an *add to with start unknown* problem type that reviews two-digit addition with one composition. Ask students to think about whether they know the parts or the whole and one part. This will guide them towards the recognition that the situation equation ___ − 27 = 45 can be written as a solution equation, 45 + 27 = ___.

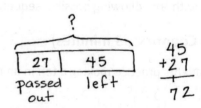

He had 72 pencils in the beginning.

Fluency Practice (10 minutes)

- Place Value **2.NBT.1, 2.NBT.3**   (3 minutes)
- Say Ten Counting **2.NBT.1**   (3 minutes)
- Compensation **2.NBT.5, 2.NBT.7**   (4 minutes)

Place Value (3 minutes)

Note: This fluency reviews place value concepts from G2–Module 3 to prepare students for this lesson's content.

    T: (Write 157 on the board.) Say the number in standard form.

    S: 157.

    T: Say 157 in unit form.

    S: 1 hundred 5 tens 7 ones.

COMMON CORE™

Lesson 11: Use math drawings to represent additions with up to two
compositions and relate drawing to the addition algorithm.
Date: 10/23/13

5.B.40

T: Say the unit form with only tens and ones.

S: 15 tens 7 ones.

T: Say the unit form with only hundreds and ones.

S: 1 hundred 57 ones.

T: Say 157 in expanded form.

S: 100 + 50 + 7.

T: How many ones are in 157?

S: 157 ones.

T: How many tens are in 157?

S: 15 tens.

T: What digit is in the ones place?

S: 7.

T: What is the value of the digit in the tens place?

S: 50.

T: What is 1 less than 157?

S: 156.

T: What is 1 more than 157?

S: 158.

Continue with the following possible sequence: 10 less? 10 more? 100 more? 100 less?

Say Ten Counting (3 minutes)

Note: Students practice making a ten in unit form to prepare for composing a ten on the place value chart in the lesson.

T: What is 3 ones + 4 ones?

S: 7 ones.

T: 6 ones + 4 ones?

S: 10 ones.

T: What is another name for 10 ones?

S: 1 ten.

T: When we make a ten, let's say the number in tens and ones. Ready? 6 ones + 5 ones.

S: 1 ten 1 one.

Repeat the process for 7 ones + 4 ones, 6 ones + 7 ones, 8 ones + 4 ones, 9 ones + 3 ones, 4 ones + 4 ones + 4 ones, 5 ones + 3 ones + 4 ones.

Compensation (4 minutes)

Note: This fluency drill reviews the mental math strategy compensation. By making a multiple of 10, students solve a much simpler addition problem. Draw a number bond for the first problem on the board to

Lesson 11:   Use math drawings to represent additions with up to two compositions and relate drawing to the addition algorithm.

Date: 10/23/13

5.B.41

help students visualize the decomposition.

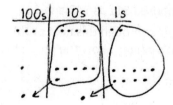

T: (Write 54 + 29 = _____.) Let's use a mental math strategy to add. How much more does 29 need to make the next ten?

S: 1 more.

T: Where can 29 get 1 more?

S: From the 54!

T: Take 1 from 54 and give it to 29. Say the new number sentence with the answer.

S: 53 + 30 = 83.

T: 39 + 46.

S: 40 + 45 = 85.

Continue with the following possible sequence: 65 + 39, 79 + 46, 128 + 52, 145 + 38, 155 + 98.

Concept Development (35 minutes)

Materials: (S) Math journals or paper

Continue checking the accuracy of student drawings. Students must attend to the proper alignment of digits, drawing number disks in clear 5-groups, and showing new groups below in the correct place. For this reason, the use of pencil and paper is more suitable than the use of a personal white board and marker.

Problem 1: 342 + 169

T: Write 342 + 169 the vertical way on your paper.

T: Let's model it by drawing chips on a place value chart. I'll make a model on the board while you make yours. Whisper-count as you draw your model.

S: (Draw chip model.) 100, 200, 300, 310, 320, 330, 340, 341, 342. (Repeat the process to show 169.)

T: Remember that we also call the written addition the *algorithm*. Use place value language to tell your partner how your model matches the algorithm.

S: 3 dots in the hundreds place is 300, 4 dots in the tens place equals 40, and 2 dots in the ones place is 2. → The model shows the Say Ten way: 3 hundreds, 4 tens, 2. → It's the same for 169, too. The model shows 1 hundred, 6 tens, 9.

T: I like the connection you made to Say Ten counting. Let's use that as we add the ones. 2 ones + 9 ones?

S: 11 ones.

T: What is 11 ones the Say Ten way?

S: 1 ten 1.

T: Tell your partner what to do first on the model and then in the algorithm.

MP.6

S: We made a ten, so we circle it! → Bundle 10 ones and draw an arrow with a new

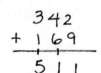

COMMON CORE   Lesson 11:   Use math drawings to represent additions with up to two
                                  compositions and relate drawing to the addition algorithm.   **5.B.42**
                     Date: 10/23/13

ten in the tens place. → Show the new unit on the line below the tens place and write 1 below the line in the ones place.

T: Yes! You composed a new unit of 10. You renamed 11 ones as 1 ten 1 one. Let's show that on our models and on the algorithm.

S: (Circle 10 ones, draw an arrow to the tens place, and add a dot to show the new unit. Write 1 on the line below the tens place and write 1 below the line in the ones place.)

T: Partners, check each other's work to be sure it matches my model and the algorithm.

T: On the algorithm, you wrote a 1 on the line. Point to what the 1 stands for on your place value model. Who can tell us?

S: (Point to the new ten on the model.) It's the new ten we drew in the tens place because we bundled 10 ones.

T: Now we add the tens. What is 4 tens + 6 tens + 1 ten?

S: 11 tens!

T: Tell your partner what to do next on the model and then in the algorithm.

MP.6

S: Circle 10 tens and draw an arrow and a dot to show the new hundred in the hundreds place. → Write 1 below the line in the tens place because there is 1 ten leftover when you compose a hundred. → Write 1 on the line below the hundreds place because we have to add a new hundred.

T: Let's show this on our models and on the algorithm.

S: (Show their work.)

T: Partners, again, check each other's work to be sure it matches my model and algorithm.

T: On the algorithm we have a 1 on the line below the hundreds place. Point to what this 1 stands for on the model. Who can tell us?

S: It's the new hundred we got when we renamed 10 tens.

T: So, 11 tens became…? The Say Ten way?

S: 1 hundred 1 ten!

T: Correct! Let's complete the problem. 3 hundreds + 1 hundred + 1 hundred is…?

S: 5 hundreds!

T: We write the digit 5 below the line in the hundreds place. Let's read the entire problem.

S: 342 + 169 = 511.

T: Talk with your partner: How does each step on the model match what we do on the algorithm?

T: Now, draw a number bond of this equation on your paper. Check your model with a partner and explain how the model matches the equation.

T: Who can explain his model to the class?

S: We add the parts to find the whole. → 342 and 169 are the parts and 511 is the whole. → I decomposed 511 as 342 and 169.

T: Now, you're going to work through this next problem while I walk around and check to see how it's going. Show the problem as a number bond as well.

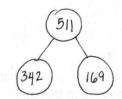

COMMON CORE   Lesson 11:   Use math drawings to represent additions with up to two compositions and relate drawing to the addition algorithm.   **5.B.43**

Date: 10/23/13

Problem 2: 545 + 278

Follow the above procedure to guide students as they write 545 + 278 vertically, model it, and solve. Remind them to be precise in lining up the digits and in drawing their number disks in neat 5-groups. Have them use place value language to explain each action they take on their model and how it is represented on the algorithm.

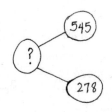

Repeat the process for 636 + 289 and 784 + 179. Continue to support struggling students, but as students demonstrate proficiency, instruct them to work on the Problem Set independently.

Problem Set (10 minutes)

Students should do their personal best to complete the Problem Set within the allotted 10 minutes. For some classes, it may be appropriate to modify the assignment by specifying which problems they work on first. Some problems do not specify a method for solving. Students solve these problems using the RDW approach used for Application Problems.

Student Debrief (10 minutes)

Lesson Objective: Use math drawings to represent additions with up to two compositions and relate drawings to the addition algorithm.

The Student Debrief is intended to invite reflection and active processing of the total lesson experience.

Invite students to review their solutions for the Problem Set. They should check work by comparing answers with a partner before going over answers as a class. Look for misconceptions or misunderstandings that can be addressed in the Debrief. Guide students in a conversation to debrief the Problem Set and process the lesson.

You may choose to use any combination of the questions below to lead the discussion.

NOTES ON
MULTIPLE MEANS OF
ACTION AND
EXPRESSION:

While we encourage students to learn new vocabulary and to use it during discussion, focus on their mathematical reasoning—their ability to make connections between the model and the algorithm, to notice patterns when bundling, to observe differences between models, and to draw conclusions—rather than their accuracy in language.

- For Problem 1(a), use place value language to explain to your partner how your model matches the algorithm.

- Think of the word *re-naming*. A friend says that the Say Ten answer to Problem 1(b), 424 + 288, is 6 hundreds, 10 tens, 12. How did you use bundling to rename the solution? What is your solution the Say Ten way?

- For Problem 1(c), where did you write the new ten or hundred in the addition algorithm? How did it match your chip model?

Lesson 11:	Use math drawings to represent additions with up to two compositions and relate drawing to the addition algorithm.	5.B.44
Date:	10/23/13	

- Explain to your partner how you solved Problems 2(a) and (b). What significant differences do you notice about the place value charts and the written addition for these two problems?

- How does having two three-digit addends (as opposed to two-digit) change the way you model and solve the addition problem?

- What important math vocabulary have we used recently to talk about making a new unit? (*Compose, bundle, rename, change.*)

Exit Ticket (3 minutes)

After the Student Debrief, instruct students to complete the Exit Ticket. A review of their work will help you assess the students' understanding of the concepts that were presented in the lesson today and plan more effectively for future lessons. You may read the questions aloud to the students.

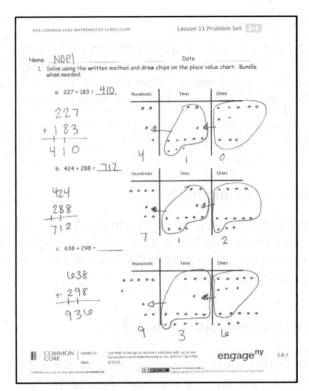

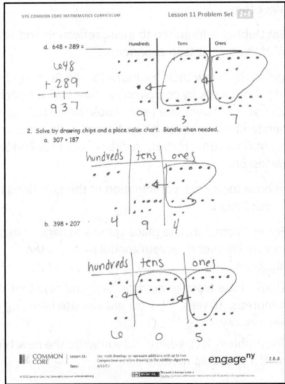

COMMON CORE™

Lesson 11:   Use math drawings to represent additions with up to two compositions and relate drawing to the addition algorithm.

Date: 10/23/13

5.B.45

Name _____   Date _____

1. Solve using the written method and draw chips on the place value chart. Bundle when needed.

Hundreds	Tens	Ones

a. 227 + 183 = _____

Hundreds	Tens	Ones

b. 424 + 288 = _____

Hundreds	Tens	Ones

c. 638 + 298 = _____

COMMON CORE

Lesson 11:   Use math drawings to represent additions with up to two compositions and relate drawing to the addition algorithm.

Date: 10/23/13

5.B.46

Hundreds	Tens	Ones

d. 648 + 289 = _____

2. Solve by drawing chips and a place value chart. Bundle when needed.

a. 307 + 187

b. 398 + 207

Lesson 11:   Use math drawings to represent additions with up to two
compositions and relate drawing to the addition algorithm.

Date: 10/23/13

5.B.47

Name _____   Date _____

Solve by drawing chips and a place value chart. Bundle when needed.

1. 267 + 356 = _____

2. 623 + 279 = _____

COMMON CORE™

Lesson 11:   Use math drawings to represent additions with up to two
                      compositions and relate drawing to the addition algorithm.

Date: 10/23/13

5.B.48

© 2013 Common Core, Inc. All rights reserved. **commoncore.org**

Name _____   Date _____

1. Solve using the written method and draw chips on the place value chart. Bundle when needed.

Hundreds	Tens	Ones

a. 167 + 224 = _____

Hundreds	Tens	Ones

b. 518 + 245 = _____

Hundreds	Tens	Ones

c. 482 + 369 = _____

COMMON CORE™ | **Lesson 11:**   Use math drawings to represent additions with up to two compositions and relate drawing to the addition algorithm.   **Date:**   10/23/13

5.B.49

Hundreds	Tens	Ones

d. 638 + 298 = _____

2. Solve by drawing chips and a place value chart. Bundle when needed.
   a. 456 + 378

   b. 187 + 567

Lesson 12

Objective: Choose and explain solution strategies and record with a written addition method.

Suggested Lesson Structure

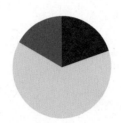

■	Fluency Practice	(12 minutes)
■	Concept Development	(38 minutes)
■	Student Debrief	(10 minutes)
	Total Time	**(60 minutes)**

Fluency Practice (12 minutes)

- Compensation **2.NBT.7**   (4 minutes)
- Sprint: Compensation Addition **2.NBT.7**   (8 minutes)

Compensation (4 minutes)

Note: This fluency drill reviews the mental math strategy, compensation. By making a multiple of 10, students solve a much simpler addition problem. Draw a number bond for the first problem on the board to help students visualize the decomposition.

> T: (Write 61 + 99 = _____.) Let's use a mental math strategy to add.
>   How much more does 99 need to make the next ten?
> S: 1 more.
> T: Where can 99 get 1 more?
> S: From the 61!
> T: Take 1 from 61 and give it to 99. Say the new number
>   sentence, with the answer.
> S: 60 + 100 = 160.
> T: 99 + 46.
> S: 100 + 45 = 145.

$$61 + 99$$
$$60 \quad 1$$
$$60 + 100 = 150$$

Continue with the following possible sequence: 99 + 38, 98 + 56, 47 + 98, 26 + 98, 54 + 99, 54 + 199, 73 + 199.

Sprint: Compensation Addition (8 minutes)

Materials: (S) Compensation Addition Sprint

Note: Students review compensation when adding in order to gain automaticity.

| **COMMON CORE** | Lesson 12: | Choose and explain solution strategies and record with a written addition method. | 5.B.51 |
| | Date: | 10/23/13 | |

Concept Development (38 minutes)

Materials: (S) Number disks (9 hundreds, 18 tens, 18 ones), personal white boards

Note: The following lesson is designed to help facilitate a discussion about choosing the most efficient problem-solving strategies. Based on student need and class ability, strategies other than those listed below may be used to solve.

Problem 1: 374 + 210

T: Turn and talk: What are some strategies you could use to solve this problem?

S: I used mental math and place value strategies. → I can write the algorithm without disks. → Arrow notation.

Instruct students to choose a written strategy that they prefer and find most efficient. Encourage students to solve independently, and circulate to provide support. Then, invite a few students to share their work and to explain how they applied the specific solution strategy. Remind students who used the written addition to keep explanations brief.

S1: I used mental math and what I know about place value. I started at 374, and then in my head I counted on 2 more hundreds. So, I had 574. Then I added a ten, and I had 584.

S2: I wrote the problem vertically and added ones, then tens, then hundreds under the line. It was easy to use the algorithm; I didn't even need to make a new ten or hundred.

S3: I used arrow notation to show the change as I added. I started with 374 and added 200, so I drew an arrow to 574. Then I added on 10 more and drew an arrow to 584.

T: Turn and talk: Now that you've heard different solution strategies, which method do you prefer for this problem and why?

S: I like the arrow way best because 210 only has hundreds and tens, so it is easy to break apart and add on. → The chip model and number disks take longer than using the arrow way. Plus, we don't have to bundle in this problem. → Now that we understand place value, it's easy to solve mentally.

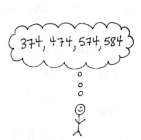

T: I'm noticing that nobody suggested a number bond for this problem. Why not?

S: None of the numbers are close to making the next hundred. → It's too hard to think of adding on to 374 to make 400. → I would have used a number bond if 374 had been 394.

T: I like the way you're thinking! Let's take a look at another problem.

COMMON CORE

Lesson 12: Choose and explain solution strategies and record with a written addition method.
Date: 10/23/13

5.B.52

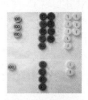

Problem 2: 398 + 142

T: Turn and talk: What are some strategies you could use to solve this problem?

S: Number disks and the vertical addition. → A number bond. → Arrow notation.

Again, instruct students to choose a written strategy that they prefer and find most efficient. Encourage them to solve independently, and circulate to provide support. Then, invite a few different students to share their work and to explain how they applied the specific solution strategy. Again, remind students who used the written addition to keep explanations brief.

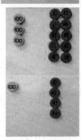

S1: I counted the disks to show both parts. I started by adding my ones. When I made a ten, I exchanged 10 ones for 1 ten. Then I added my tens. When I made a hundred, I exchanged 10 tens for a hundred. Then I added my hundreds. The answer is 540.

MP.3

S2: I know that 398 is very close to 400 so I used a number bond. I decomposed 142 into 140 and 2. Then, I bonded the 2 with 398 to make 400, and 400 plus 140 equals 540.

S3: I like arrow notation because you can start with 398 and first add 2, so 400, then add 100, then 40 more, and you have 540.

T: Turn and talk: Which method do you think is best for this problem and why?

S: Making a hundred is the easiest and quickest, especially since you only needed to add on 2. → Using the chip model is good, but it was faster to break apart the 142. → I prefer the arrow way because once you add 2 to make 400, it's easy to add a hundred and 4 tens.

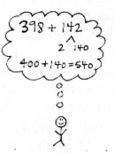

Problem 3: 287 + 234

Note: For this problem, some students may choose to represent the problem using number disks or drawings, while others may choose to solve using only the algorithm. Although the most efficient strategy will most likely be using the algorithm, the Grade 2 expectation is not that students use the algorithm alone, but that they use it in conjunction with a representation.

T: Turn and talk: What are some strategies you could use to solve this problem?

S: A number disk drawing. → I would write just using the algorithm.

Students follow the same procedure as suggested in Problems 1 and 2. Since this problem does not lend itself to other simplifying strategies, invite one, maybe two, students to share.

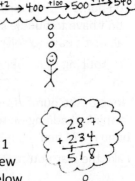

S: My model shows that 11 ones becomes 1 ten, 1 one. I showed that by writing 1 on the line below the tens place. 11 tens plus 1 ten is 12 tens, so I showed a new hundred, and then I wrote a 1 on the line below the hundreds place and a 2 below the line in the tens place. Then I just added my hundred. So the answer is 621.

T: How was this the most efficient way to solve this problem? Why didn't you

 COMMON CORE™   Lesson 12:   Choose and explain solution strategies and record with a written addition method.   **5.B.53**

Date: 10/23/13

choose a simplifying strategy?

S: Because solving using the arrow way would be too complicated. → The make a hundred strategy doesn't make it easier because the numbers are too far from the closest hundred. → Since you have to bundle twice, I like using the chips and the algorithm.

T: Now you're going to have the chance to analyze some student work and to solve some problems by choosing a written strategy that works best for you.

Problem Set (10 minutes)

Students should do their personal best to complete the Problem Set within the allotted 10 minutes. For some classes, it may be appropriate to modify the assignment by specifying which problems they work on first. Some problems do not specify a method for solving. Students solve these problems using the RDW approach used for Application Problems.

Student Debrief (10 minutes)

Lesson Objective: Choose and explain solution strategies and record with a written addition method.

The Student Debrief is intended to invite reflection and active processing of the total lesson experience.

Invite students to review their solutions for the Problem Set. They should check work by comparing answers with a partner before going over answers as a class. Look for misconceptions or misunderstandings that can be addressed in the Debrief. Guide students in a conversation to debrief the Problem Set and process the lesson.

You may choose to use any combination of the questions below to lead the discussion.

- Share with your partner: Which strategy was most efficient for Tracy to use? Why? Do you agree or disagree with your partner?
- Can you explain any alternate problem-solving strategies for Problem 1?
- For Problem 2(a), which strategy did you choose to solve? Why?
- For Problem 2(b), which strategy did you choose to solve? How did your understanding of place value help you to solve this problem quickly?

NOTES ON MULTIPLE MEANS OF ENGAGEMENT:

Writing about math can be daunting for some students.

- Provide oral options for informal assessment on the Problem Set rather than writing.
- Before they begin writing, ask students questions to probe what they mean.
- Support written responses on the Problem Set by helping students get started. For example, "The number bond was the best strategy because...."

NOTES ON MULTIPLE MEANS OF REPRESENTATION:

During the Debrief, invite students to share exemplary explanations with the whole class. Encourage students to model alternative, even creative, solutions. For example, for Problem 1 on the Problem Set (299 + 399), a student might suggest adding hundreds and then subtracting 2: "If you add 1 to 299 and 399, you get 300 + 400 equals 700. Then, you have to subtract 2 from 700, so 698."

- How did you solve Problem 2(c)? What made 2(c) more difficult to solve with a simplifying strategy? Could you have done so?

Exit Ticket (3 minutes)

After the Student Debrief, instruct students to complete the Exit Ticket. A review of their work will help you assess the students' understanding of the concepts that were presented in the lesson today and plan more effectively for future lessons. You may read the questions aloud to the students.

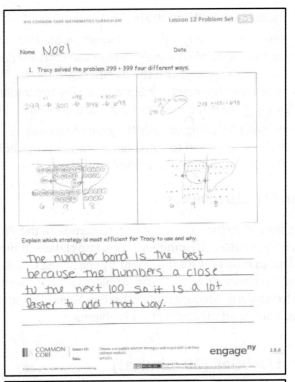

Lesson 12: Choose and explain solution strategies and record with a written addition method.

Date: 10/23/13

5.B.55

A

Add.

Correct _____

1	98 + 3 =		23	99 + 12 =	
2	98 + 4 =		24	99 + 23 =	
3	98 + 5 =		25	99 + 34 =	
4	98 + 8 =		26	99 + 45 =	
5	98 + 6 =		27	99 + 56 =	
6	98 + 9 =		28	99 + 67 =	
7	98 + 7 =		29	99 + 78 =	
8	99 + 2 =		30	35 + 99 =	
9	99 + 3 =		31	45 + 98 =	
10	99 + 4 =		32	46 + 99 =	
11	99 + 9 =		33	56 + 98 =	
12	99 + 6 =		34	67 + 99 =	
13	99 + 8 =		35	77 + 98 =	
14	99 + 5 =		36	68 + 99 =	
15	99 + 7 =		37	78 + 98 =	
16	98 + 13 =		38	99 + 95 =	
17	98 + 24 =		39	93 + 99 =	
18	98 + 35 =		40	99 + 95 =	
19	98 + 46 =		41	94 + 99 =	
20	98 + 57 =		42	98 + 96 =	
21	98 + 68 =		43	94 + 98 =	
22	98 + 79 =		44	98 + 88 =	

© Bill Davidson

B   Improvement _____   # Correct _____

Add.

1	99 + 2 =		23	98 + 13 =	
2	99 + 3 =		24	98 + 24 =	
3	99 + 4 =		25	98 + 35 =	
4	99 + 8 =		26	98 + 46 =	
5	99 + 6 =		27	98 + 57 =	
6	99 + 9 =		28	98 + 68 =	
7	99 + 5 =		29	98 + 79 =	
8	99 + 7 =		30	25 + 99 =	
9	98 + 3 =		31	35 + 98 =	
10	98 + 4 =		32	36 + 99 =	
11	98 + 5 =		33	46 + 98 =	
12	98 + 9 =		34	57 + 99 =	
13	98 + 7 =		35	67 + 98 =	
14	98 + 8 =		36	78 + 99 =	
15	98 + 6 =		37	88 + 98 =	
16	99 + 12 =		38	99 + 93 =	
17	99 + 23 =		39	95 + 99 =	
18	99 + 34 =		40	99 + 97 =	
19	99 + 45 =		41	92 + 99 =	
20	99 + 56 =		42	98 + 94 =	
21	99 + 67 =		43	96 + 98 =	
22	99 + 78 =		44	98 + 86 =	

© Bill Davidson

COMMON CORE   Lesson 12:   Choose and explain solution strategies and record with a written addition method.
Date: 10/23/13   5.B.57

Name _____   Date _____

1. Tracy solved the problem 299 + 399 four different ways.

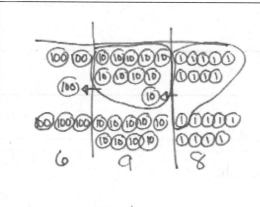

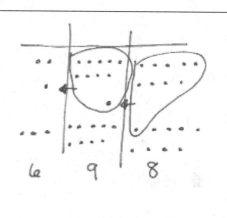

Explain which strategy is most efficient for Tracy to use and why.

_____

_____

_____

_____

_____

COMMON CORE   Lesson 12:   Choose and explain solution strategies and record with a written
                 addition method.   5.B.58
                 Date: 10/23/13

2. Choose the best strategy and solve. Explain why you chose that strategy.

a. 221 + 498	Explanation: _____ _____ _____ _____
b. 467 + 200	Explanation: _____ _____ _____ _____
c. 378 + 464	Explanation: _____ _____ _____ _____

Name _____   Date _____

Choose the best strategy and solve. Explain why you chose that strategy.

1. 467 + 298	Explanation: _____ _____ _____ _____
2. 300 + 524	Explanation: _____ _____ _____ _____

Name _____   Date _____

1. Solve 435 + 290 using two different strategies.

a.	b.

Explain which strategy would be easier and why.

_____

_____

_____

_____

COMMON CORE   Lesson 12:   Choose and explain solution strategies and record with a written
                                   addition method.
                    Date: 10/23/13   5.B.61

© 2013 Common Core, Inc. All rights reserved. **commoncore.org**

2. Choose the best strategy and solve. Explain why you chose that strategy.

a. 299 + 458	Explanation:
	_____
	_____
	_____
	_____
b. 733 + 210	Explanation:
	_____
	_____
	_____
	_____
c. 295 + 466	Explanation:
	_____
	_____
	_____
	_____

Topic C

Strategies for Decomposing Tens and Hundreds Within 1,000

2.NBT.7, 2.NBT.9

Focus Standard:	2.NBT.7	Add and subtract within 1000, using concrete models or drawings and strategies based on place value, properties of operations, and/or the relationship between addition and subtraction; relate the strategy to a written method. Understand that in adding or subtracting three-digit numbers, one adds or subtracts hundreds and hundreds, tens and tens, ones and ones; and sometimes it is necessary to compose or decompose tens or hundreds.
	2.NBT.9	Explain why addition and subtraction strategies work, using place value and the properties of operations. (Explanations may be supported by drawings or objects.)
Instructional Days:	6	
Coherence -Links from:	G2–M4	Addition and Subtraction Within 200 with Word Problems to 100
-Links to:	G3–M2	Place Value and Problem Solving with Units of Measure
	G4–M1	Place Value, Rounding, and Algorithms for Addition and Subtraction

Topic C builds upon Module 4's groundwork, now decomposing tens and hundreds within 1,000 (**2.NBT.7**). In Lesson 13, students model decompositions with number disks on their place value charts while simultaneously recording these changes in the written vertical form. Students draw a magnifying glass around the minuend, as they did in Module 4. They then ask the familiar questions: *Do I have enough ones to subtract? Do I have enough tens?* When the answer is *no*, students exchange one of the larger units for ten of the smaller units. They record the change in the algorithm, following this procedure for each place on the place value chart.

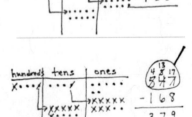

In Lessons 14 and 15, students transition to making math drawings, thus completing the move from concrete to pictorial representations. They follow the same procedure for decomposing numbers as in Lesson 13, but now they use number disk drawings (Lesson 14) and chip models (Lesson 15). Students continue to record changes in the vertical method as they relate their drawings to the algorithm, and they use place value reasoning and the properties of operations to solve problems with up to two decompositions (e.g., 547 – 168, as shown above).

Lessons 16 and 17 focus on the special case of subtracting from multiples of 100 and numbers with zero in the tens place. Students recall the decomposition of 100 and 200 in Module 4 in one or two steps, using the same reasoning to subtract from larger numbers. For example, 300 can be decomposed into 2 hundreds and 10 tens, then 1 ten is decomposed into 10 ones (two steps); or 300 can be renamed directly as 2 hundreds, 9 tens, and 10 ones (one step). In each case, students use math drawings to model the decompositions and relate them to the written vertical form, step by step.

In Lesson 18, students work with three-digit subtraction problems, which they apply multiple strategies to solve. For example, with 300 – 247, students learn they can use compensation to subtract 1 from each number, making the equivalent expression 299 – 246, which requires no renaming. They may also use the related addition sentence, 247 + ___ = 300, and then use arrow notation to solve, counting up 3 to 250 and then adding on 50, to find the answer of 53. For some problems, such as 507 – 359, students may choose to draw a chip model and relate it to the algorithm, renaming 507 as 4 hundreds, 9 tens, 17 ones in one step. As students apply alternate methods, the emphasis is placed on students explaining and critiquing various strategies.

A Teaching Sequence Towards Mastery of Strategies for Decomposing Tens and Hundreds Within 1,000
Objective 1: Relate manipulative representations to the subtraction algorithm, and use addition to explain why the subtraction method works. (Lesson 13)
Objective 2: Use math drawings to represent subtraction with up to two decompositions, relate drawings to the algorithm, and use addition to explain why the subtraction method works. (Lessons 14–15)
Objective 3: Subtract from multiples of 100 and from numbers with zero in the tens place. (Lessons 16–17)
Objective 4: Apply and explain alternate methods for subtracting from multiples of 100 and from numbers with zero in the tens place. (Lesson 18)

Lesson 13

Objective: Relate manipulative representations to the subtraction algorithm, and use addition to explain why the subtraction method works.

Suggested Lesson Structure

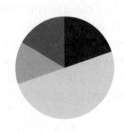

▨ Application Problem	(8 minutes)
■ Fluency Practice	(12 minutes)
▨ Concept Development	(30 minutes)
▨ Student Debrief	(10 minutes)
Total Time	**(60 minutes)**

Application Problem (8 minutes)

A fruit seller buys a carton of 90 apples.

Finding that 18 of them are rotten, he throws them away.

He sells 22 of the ones that are left on Monday. How many apples does he have left to sell?

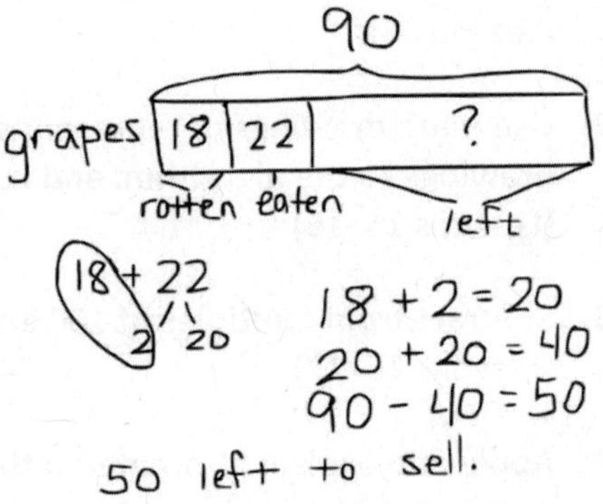

Note: This problem is designed for independent practice. Possibly encourage students to use the RDW process without dictating what to draw. Two-step problems challenge students to think through the first step before moving on to the second. The number sentences can help them to see and articulate the steps as well.

(handwritten work):

90

grapes | 18 | 22 | ? |
rotten   eaten   left

18 + 22
  /\
 2 20

18 + 2 = 20
20 + 20 = 40
90 − 40 = 50

50 left to sell.

Fluency Practice (12 minutes)

- Making the Next Ten **2.OA.2, 2.NBT.5**   (5 minutes)
- Making the Next Hundred **2.NBT.5, 2.NBT.7**   (5 minutes)
- Subtracting Multiples of Hundreds and Tens **2.NBT.5, 2.NBT.7**   (2 minutes)

Making the Next Ten (5 minutes)

Materials: (S) Personal white boards

Note: This fluency will review foundations that lead into today's lesson.

   T: When I say 9 + 4, you write 10 + 3. Ready? 9 + 4.

COMMON CORE™   Lesson 13:   Relate manipulative representations to the subtraction algorithm, and   5.C.3
use addition to explain why the subtraction method works.
Date: 10/23/13

S: 10 + 3.

T: Tell me the number sentence with the answer.

S: 10 + 3 = 13.

T: Write the related addition sentence starting with 9 + 4.

S: 9 + 4 = 13.

Continue with the following possible sequence: 19 + 4, 9 + 6, 19 + 6, 8 + 3, 18 + 3, 8 + 5, 18 + 5, 7 + 6, 17 + 6, 7 + 4, 17 + 4, 9 + 5, 19 + 5, 8 + 6, 18 + 6, 8 + 7, 17 + 8.

Making the Next Hundred (5 minutes)

Note: This fluency will review foundations that lead into today's lesson.

T: (Write 170 on the board.) Let's find missing part to make the next hundred. What is the next hundred?

S: 200.

T: If I say 170, you say the missing number needed to make 200. Ready? 170.

S: 30.

T: Tell me the addition sentence.

S: 170 + 30 = 200.

Continue with the following possible sequence: 190, 160, 260, 270, 370, 380, 580, 620, 720, 740, 940, 194, 196, 216, 214, 224.

Subtracting Multiples of Hundreds and Tens (2 minutes)

Note: Students review fluently subtracting multiples of tens and hundreds in preparation for the lesson.

T: What is 2 tens less than 130?

S: 110.

T: Give the subtraction number sentence.

S: 130 − 20 = 110.

T: What is 2 hundreds less than 350?

S: 150.

T: Give the subtraction number sentence.

S: 350 − 200 = 150.

Continue with the following sequence: 6 tens less than 150, 3 hundreds less than 550, 7 tens less than 250, 6 tens less than 340, 4 hundreds less than 880.

Concept Development (30 minutes)

Materials: (T) Number disks (19 ones, 19 tens, 10 hundreds), place value chart (S) Number disks (19 ones, 19 tens, and 10 hundreds), place value charts, personal white boards

Lesson 13:   Relate manipulative representations to the subtraction algorithm, and use addition to explain why the subtraction method works.

Date: 10/23/13

       5.C.4

Problem 1: 244 – 121

T: (Write 244 – 121 on the board.) Read this problem with me.

T/S: (Read the problem chorally.) 244 minus 121.

T: (Draw a blank number bond on the board.) How would you complete this number bond? Talk to a partner and use part–whole language.

S: I would put 244 in the whole and 121 in one part. → I know 244 is the whole, since we are subtracting.

T: Great! What do we need to show on our place value charts? Talk to your neighbor.

S: We only show the whole when subtracting. → We are going to show 244, because it's the whole. → We are going to start with 244 and then take away 21.

T: Count in unit form as I place the disks. 1 hundred, 2 hundreds, 2 hundreds 1 ten, 2 hundreds 2 tens, 2 hundreds 3 tens, …2 hundred 4 tens 4 ones. (Place 2 hundreds, 4 tens, and 4 ones on your place value chart. Direct students to do the same.)

T: Today, as we solve subtraction problems, we are going to record our work vertically. (Write the problem in vertical form.)

T: Remember our magnifying glasses! Let's draw an imaginary magnifying glass around 244, since that is the whole. (Draw the magnifying glass around 244.)

T: Like a detective, look carefully at each place to see if we have enough units to subtract moving from the smallest unit to the largest. (Give students a moment to check.)

T: Are we ready to subtract in the ones, tens, and hundreds?

S: Yes!

T: Go for it!

Have students remove 1 hundred, 2 tens, and 1 one from their place value charts and record the subtraction using the written method.

T: What is 244 – 121?

S: 123.

T: (Write 123 in the missing part in the number bond.)

T: Now, using our number bond, I bet it's easy for someone to come up with a related addition problem to check our answer. What problem should we write?

S: 123 + 121.

T: Solve this problem on your boards and turn them over when you have the answer.

T: What is the sum?

S: 244!

T: It worked!

NOTES ON MULTIPLE MEANS OF ACTION AND EXPRESSION:

Students may remark upon the sequence of the digits in 123. Encourage the excitement some may feel about finding the pattern in the numbers.

Lesson 13:   Relate manipulative representations to the subtraction algorithm, and use addition to explain why the subtraction method works.

Date: 10/23/13

5.C.5

Problem 2: 244 – 125

T: Let's try another problem together. This time I want you to record your work as I do mine. (Write 244 – 125 on the board in vertical form. Students do the same.)

T: What should we do first?

S: Find out if we need to unbundle. → Look at the numbers to see if we can solve mentally.

T: True! For this problem, let's solve using the algorithm. Show me the whole using your number disks.

S: (Represent 244 using number disks on their place value charts.)

T: (Draw the magnifying glass with enough space to write renaming, and instruct students to do the same.)

T: Okay, I'm looking closely. Where do we start?

S: Start in the ones column. → Check to see if you can subtract the ones.

T: Can we subtract 5 ones from 4 ones?

S: No!

T: What should we do?

S: Decompose a ten. → Rename a ten as ten ones. → Add 10 ones to 4 ones, so we have 14 ones.

T: Okay, go ahead and show that change using your disks. (Change a ten for 10 ones. Arrange them in 5-groups on your place value chart.)

MP.6

T: Whatever we do to our number disks, we must also do on the vertical subtraction. How should we record unbundling a ten?

S: Cross out 4 tens and write 3 tens above it. → Cross out the 4 in the ones place and write 14 above it. → Change 4 tens to 3 tens and 4 ones to 14 ones.

T: Now, how many tens and ones do we have on our charts?

S: 3 tens, 14 ones.

T: Look at each column closely. Tell me, are we ready to subtract?

S: Yes!

T: Then let's subtract!

T: What is the answer to 244 – 125?

S: 119.

T: Check your answer with addition. Write a complete number bond. Does it work? (Pause to give students time to work.)

S: Yes!

NOTES ON MULTIPLE MEANS OF REPRESENTATION:

Some students may benefit from recording a new group of 10 differently. For example, while most will likely cross out the 4 in the ones place and write a 14 above it, others may internalize the change by crossing out the 4 and writing 10 + 4 above it, then subtracting 10 – 5 and adding 4 to make 9 ones.

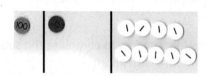

   Lesson 13:   Relate manipulative representations to the subtraction algorithm, and
                                 use addition to explain why the subtraction method works.
                 Date: 10/23/13

© 2013 Common Core, Inc. All rights reserved. commoncore.org

5.C.6

Problem 3: 312 – 186

T: Let's try another problem together. (Write 312 – 186 on the board in vertical form. Allow students time to do the same.) I'm going to follow what you do.

T: What is different about this problem?

S: We are taking away hundreds too. → We are subtracting three digits. → You need to unbundle tens *and* hundreds in this problem.

T: Let's see if we need to unbundle. Do we have enough ones?

S: No!

T: Do we have enough tens?

S: No!

T: Let's unbundle to get ready to subtract. What should we do?

S: Change a ten for 10 ones. → Rename a ten as 10 ones. → Decompose a ten to make more ones.

T: (Change a ten for 10 ones.) Are we ready to subtract in the ones place?

T: How many ones do we have now?

S: 12!

T: How many tens?

S: None! → Zero!

T: Let's record this on our written subtraction. (shown at right).

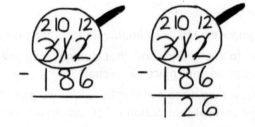

T: Are we ready to subtract in the tens place?

S: No!

T: Obviously! What should we do now?

S: Unbundle a hundred! → Rename a hundred as 10 tens. → Break open a hundred to make 10 tens.

T: (Change a hundred for 10 tens.) How many tens do we have now?

S: 10!

T: How many hundreds?

S: 2!

T: Let's write this on our algorithm (shown at right).

T: Are we ready to subtract 186 from 312?

S: Yes!

Allow time for students to complete the subtraction independently, write a complete number bond, and check their work with addition.

Lesson 13:   Relate manipulative representations to the subtraction algorithm, and
               use addition to explain why the subtraction method works.
Date: 10/23/13

5.C.7

Problem Set (10 minutes)

Students should do their personal best to complete the Problem Set within the allotted 10 minutes. For some classes, it may be appropriate to modify the assignment by specifying which problems they work on first. Some problems do not specify a method for solving. Students solve these problems using the RDW approach used for Application Problems.

Student Debrief (10 minutes)

Lesson Objective: Relate manipulative representations to the subtraction algorithm, and use addition to explain why the subtraction method works.

The Student Debrief is intended to invite reflection and active processing of the total lesson experience.

Invite students to review their solutions for the Problem Set. They should check work by comparing answers with a partner before going over answers as a class. Look for misconceptions or misunderstandings that can be addressed in the Debrief. Guide students in a conversation to debrief the Problem Set and process the lesson.

You may choose to use any combination of the questions below to lead the discussion.

- What pattern did you notice in Problems 1(a) and (b)?
- For Problems 2(a) and (b), which problems were you able to solve mentally? Why?
- For Problem 2(c), how is it possible that both problems have the same difference?
- Explain to your partner how you used number disks to solve Problem 2(d). How did your work with the number disks match the vertical subtraction?
- For each Problem in 2(e), did you change 1 hundred for 10 tens or 1 ten for 10 ones? How did you show the change using the algorithm?
- How did you use addition today to explain why the subtraction works? Use part–whole language to explain your thinking.

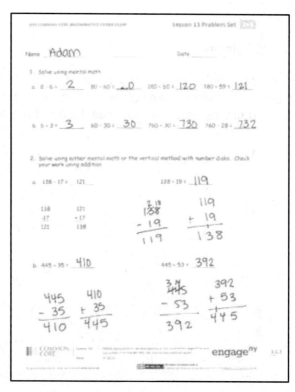

Lesson 13: Relate manipulative representations to the subtraction algorithm, and use addition to explain why the subtraction method works.

Date: 10/23/13

5.C.8

Exit Ticket (3 minutes)

After the Student Debrief, instruct students to complete the Exit Ticket. A review of their work will help you assess the students' understanding of the concepts that were presented in the lesson today and plan more effectively for future lessons. You may read the questions aloud to the students.

Lesson 13:   Relate manipulative representations to the subtraction algorithm, and
              use addition to explain why the subtraction method works.
Date: 10/23/13

5.C.9

Name _____   Date _____

1. Solve using mental math.

    a. 8 – 6 = _____   80 – 60 = _____   180 – 60 = _____   180 – 59 = _____

    b. 6 – 3 = _____   60 – 30 = _____   760 – 30 = _____   760 – 28 = _____

2. Solve using either mental math or the vertical method with number disks. Check your work using addition.

    a.   138 – 17 = ___121___   138 – 19 = _____

         138   121
         -17   + 17
         121   138

    b. 445 – 35 = _____   445 – 53 = _____

c. 863 – 170 = _____   845 – 152 = _____

d. 472 – 228 = _____   418 – 274 = _____

e. 567 – 184 = _____   567 – 148 = _____

Lesson 13:   Relate manipulative representations to the subtraction algorithm, and
use addition to explain why the subtraction method works.
Date: 10/23/13

5.C.11

Name _____   Date _____

Solve using either mental math or the vertical method with number disks. Check your work using addition.

1. 378 – 117 = _____   378 – 119 = _____

2. 853 – 433 = _____   853 – 548 = _____

Lesson 13:   Relate manipulative representations to the subtraction algorithm, and
use addition to explain why the subtraction method works.

Date: 10/23/13

5.C.12

Name _____   Date _____

1. Solve using mental math.

    a. 9 – 5 = _____   90 – 50 = _____   190 – 50 = _____   190 – 49 = _____

    b. 7 – 4 = _____   70 – 40 = _____   370 – 40 = _____   370 – 39 = _____

2. Solve using either mental math or the vertical method with number disks. Check your work using addition.

    a. 153 – 31 = __122__   153 – 38 = _____

```
153          122
-31         + 31
122          153
```

    b. 362 – 49 = _____   485 – 177 = _____

COMMON CORE™   Lesson 13:   Relate manipulative representations to the subtraction algorithm, and   5.C.13
                               use addition to explain why the subtraction method works.
                     Date: 10/23/13

c. 753 – 290 = _____   567 – 290 = _____

d. 873 – 428 = _____   817 – 565 = _____

e. 973 – 681 = _____   748 – 239 = _____

3. Complete the number sentence modeled by disks.

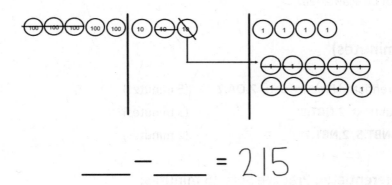

_____ – _____ = 215

Lesson 13:   Relate manipulative representations to the subtraction algorithm, and
             use addition to explain why the subtraction method works.   5.C.14

Date: 10/23/13

Lesson 14

Objective: Use math drawings to represent subtraction with up to two decompositions, relate drawings to the algorithm, and use addition to explain why the subtraction method works.

Suggested Lesson Structure

■	Application Problem	(8 minutes)
■	Fluency Practice	(12 minutes)
■	Concept Development	(30 minutes)
■	Student Debrief	(10 minutes)
	Total Time	**(60 minutes)**

Application Problem (8 minutes)

Brienne has 23 fewer pennies than Alonzo. Alonzo has 45 pennies.

    a. How many pennies does Brienne have?

    b. How many pennies do Alonzo and Brienne have altogether?

Note: This problem is intended for guided practice to help students gain familiarity with the *compare with smaller unknown* problem type. The numbers are intentionally small to allow students to focus on the relationship between the numbers. This also serves as a bridge to later work with two-step problems where the second step will not be scaffolded.

Drawing of tape diagrams:

A [45]
B [? | 23]
    fewer

45 − 23 = ☐
23 + ☐ = 45

Brienne has 22 pennies.

[45 | 22] with ? above
45 + 22 = ☐

They have 67 pennies altogether.

Fluency Practice (12 minutes)

- Grade 2 Core Fluency Differentiated Practice Sets   **2.OA.2**   (5 minutes)
- Using the Nearest Ten to Subtract   **2.NBT.5**   (5 minutes)
- Subtract Common Units   **2.NBT.5, 2.NBT.7**   (2 minutes)

Grade 2 Core Fluency Differentiated Practice Sets (5 minutes)

Materials: (S) Core Fluency Practice Sets

	Lesson 14:	Use math drawings to represent subtraction with up to two decompositions, relate drawings to the algorithm, and use addition to explain why the subtraction method works.	**5.C.15**
	Date:	10/23/13	

Note: During Topic C and for the remainder of the year, each day's fluency includes an opportunity for review and mastery of the sums and differences with totals through 20 by means of the Core Fluency Practice Sets or Sprints. Five options are provided in this lesson for the Core Fluency Practice Set, with Sheet A being the most simple addition fluency of the grade to Sheet E being the most complex. Start all students on Sheet A. Keep a record of student progress so that you can move students to more complex sheets when they are ready.

Students complete as many problems as they can in 120 seconds. We recommend 100% accuracy and completion before moving to the next level. Collect any Practice Sheets that have been completed within the 120 seconds and check the answers. The next time Core Fluency Practice Sets are used, students who have successfully completed their set today can be provided with the next level.

Assign early finishers a counting pattern and start number. Celebrate improvement as well as advancement. Students should be encouraged to compete with themselves rather than their peers. Discuss with students possible strategies to solve the problems. Notify caring adults of each child's progress.

Using the Nearest Ten to Subtract (5 minutes)

Note: Students use bonds of 10 when subtracting as a mental strategy to help subtract fluently with larger numbers.

  T: (Post 16 – 9 on the board.) Raise your hand when you know 16 – 9.
  S: 7.
  T: (Write in the bond.) 10 – 9 is…?
  S: 1.
  T: 1 + 6 is…?
  S: 7.

Continue with the following possible sequence: 15 – 9, 13 – 8, 15 – 7, 16 – 7, 12 – 9, 13 – 7, 23 – 7, 25 – 7, 25 – 9, 26 – 9, 27 – 9, 27 – 9, 37 – 9, 37 – 19, 35 – 19, 45 – 19, 47 – 18, 48 – 29.

Subtract Common Units (2 minutes)

Materials: (S) Personal white boards

Note: Reviewing this mental math fluency will prepare students for understanding the importance of the subtraction algorithm.

  T: (Project 77.) Say the number in unit form.
  S: 7 tens 7 ones.
  T: (Write 77 – 22 = _____.) Say the subtraction sentence and answer in unit form.
  S: 7 tens 7 ones – 2 tens 2 ones = 5 tens 5 ones.
  T: Write the subtraction sentence on your boards.

Repeat the process and continue with the following possible sequence: 88 – 33, 66 – 44, 266 – 44, 55 – 33, and 555 – 33.

　｜　Lesson 14:　　Use math drawings to represent subtraction with up to two
　　　　　　　　　　　　　　decompositions, relate drawings to the algorithm, and use addition
　　　　　　　　　　　　　　to explain why the subtraction method works.　　　　　　　　　　　　5.C.16
　　　　　　Date:　　　10/23/13

Concept Development (30 minutes)

Materials: (S) Personal white boards, math journals or paper

Note: In this lesson, students model subtraction by drawing number disks. This serves as a bridge between their use of actual place value disks in G2–M5–Lesson 13 and the chip model drawings called for in G2–M5–Lesson 15. Personal white boards can be used in place of paper as students demonstrate precision in their drawings by aligning digits in their proper place and aligning disks in 5-groups.

Problem 1: 584 – 147

T: (Write 584 – 147 horizontally.) Would it be easy to solve this problem mentally?

S: No, I can't keep all those numbers in my head. → It would be too confusing to solve mentally. → The algorithm would be the easiest way to solve.

T: Ah! Part of your job as students is to know which tools make your work easier. The algorithm is an excellent choice for a problem like this.

T: Rewrite the problem with me. (Write the problem vertically as students do the same.)

T: Now, let's make a math drawing using place value disks, because that will help us make sense of the numbers. First, tell your partner what you will draw.

S: I'll show 500, 80, and 4 with disks. → I'll draw 5 hundreds, 8 tens, and 4 ones.

T: I like the way you used place value language. Let's draw our models. Whisper-count the total as you draw the disks.

S: (Whisper-count and draw.) 100, 200, 300, …584.

T: Do we need to draw 147?

S: No, it's part of 584. → We only draw the whole when we subtract. Then we take away one part to show the other part.

T: Excellent part–whole thinking!

T: Let's set up the problem to subtract. We need to draw a…?

S: Magnifying glass! (Draw a circle around 584 as students do the same.)

T: Let's ask our questions. Are we ready to subtract in the ones place?

S: No! 4 is smaller than 7.

T: Where can we get some more ones?

S: From the tens place. → Decompose a ten. → Rename 8 tens as 7 tens 10 ones.

MP.7

> NOTES ON
> MULTIPLE MEANS OF
> ACTION AND
> EXPRESSION:
>
> Some students may answer *yes* to the question of solving the problem mentally. After all the lessons and practice with simplifying strategies, they may not need to write their work and may even resist having to do so. Encourage these students to follow along with the algorithm practice and use their mental math to check the

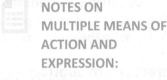

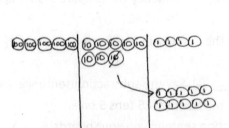

COMMON CORE   Lesson 14:   Use math drawings to represent subtraction with up to two decompositions, relate drawings to the algorithm, and use addition to explain why the subtraction method works.   5.C.17

Date: 10/23/13

T: Let's show that on our model. (Cross off 1 ten, draw an arrow to the ones place, and draw 10 ones as students do the same.)

T: Remember, as we change the model, we change the numbers in the written subtraction.

T: Looking at our model, how many tens do we have now?

S: 7 tens!

T: So, we cross off the 8 tens and write 7 tens. (Record the change as students do the same.)

T: How many ones do you see now?

S: 14 ones!

T: Let's cross off the 4 ones and write 14 ones. (Record the change as students do the same.)

MP.7

T: Look at the tens place. Are we ready to subtract in the tens place?

S: Yes, because 7 is greater than 4.

T: Are we ready to subtract in the hundreds place?

S: Yes!

T: Why?

S: 500 is greater than 100!

T: Now, we're ready to subtract. Talk with your partner. Take turns sharing how you'll show the subtraction on your model and using the algorithm.

S: I cross off 7 ones and 7 ones are left, so I write 7 below the line in the ones place. → I cross off forty and that leaves 30, so I write 3 below the line in the tens place. → 5 hundreds minus 1 hundred is 4 hundreds. I cross off 1 hundred and 4 hundreds are left, so I write 4 below the line in the hundreds place.

T: Read the complete number sentence.

S: 584 – 147 equals 437.

T: How can we prove our answer is correct?

S: We can draw a number bond, because part + part = whole.

T: It's true that part + part = whole, but how can we prove that the part we found is correct?

S: Add the parts to see if they equal the whole. → Add 147 + 437 to see if it equals 584.

T: Draw a model to solve 147 + 437. Check your model and your vertical addition with your partner.

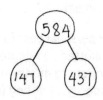

NOTES ON MULTIPLE MEANS OF ENGAGEMENT:

Some students may subtract starting in the hundreds place. Be prepared for that possibility and encourage the students to explain why that works.

Circulate to assess and support students. Project student work or call students to the board to show their model, algorithm, or number bond. Encourage students to use place value language to explain their work. Note that students began to work with chip models in G2–Module 4, and those who are confident with this more abstract model and are able to explain it may choose to use it when they work independently.

T: Who can explain why 147 + 437 helps us check 584 – 147?

S: I can show it on my chip model. You see the two parts, 147 and 437, and altogether they show 500

Lesson 14: Use math drawings to represent subtraction with up to two decompositions, relate drawings to the algorithm, and use addition to explain why the subtraction method works.

Date: 10/23/13

5.C.18

+ 80 + 4, which is 584. → I can show it on my number disk drawing. Inside 584, I can show 1 hundred, 4 tens, 7 ones, and also 4 hundreds, 3 tens, and 7 ones. → 7 ones + 7 ones equals 14 ones. That's 4 ones and a new ten. 4 tens + 3 tens + 1 ten is 8 tens. Then 1 hundred + 4 hundreds is 5 hundreds. That makes 584.

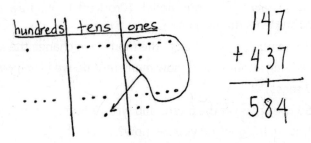

T: Those are very clear explanations using place value language. So if 584 – 147 = 437, then 437 + 147 = 584. Is this true?

S: True!

Problem 2: 637 – 253

Follow the above procedure to guide students as they write 637 – 253 vertically, model it with disks, and solve. Remind them to be precise in lining up the digits and in drawing their number disks in neat 5-groups. Have them use place value language to explain each action they take on their model and how it is represented using the algorithm. Continue to have them check their work with addition and to explain why this works.

Repeat the process for 725 – 396 and 936 – 468. If students choose to solve 725 – 396 using mental math, be sure to invite them to explain their reasoning, either at this point in the lesson or during the Debrief.

Continue to support struggling students, but as they demonstrate proficiency, instruct them to work on the Problem Set independently.

Problem Set (10 minutes)

Students should do their personal best to complete the Problem Set within the allotted 10 minutes. For some classes, it may be appropriate to modify the assignment by specifying which problems they work on first. Some problems do not specify a method for solving. Students solve these problems using the RDW approach used for Application Problems.

Student Debrief (10 minutes)

Lesson Objective: Use math drawings to represent subtraction with up to two decompositions, relate drawings to the algorithm, and use addition to explain why the subtraction method works.

Lesson 14:   Use math drawings to represent subtraction with up to two
              decompositions, relate drawings to the algorithm, and use addition
              to explain why the subtraction method works.

Date: 10/23/13

5.C.19

The Student Debrief is intended to invite reflection and active processing of the total lesson experience.

Invite students to review their solutions for the Problem Set. They should check work by comparing answers with a partner before going over answers as a class. Look for misconceptions or misunderstandings that can be addressed in the Debrief. Guide students in a conversation to debrief the Problem Set and process the lesson.

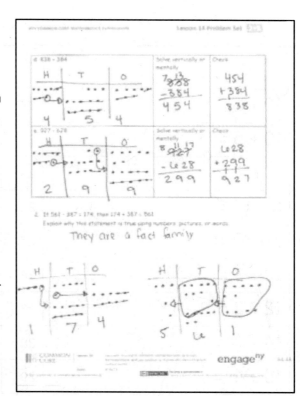

You may choose to use any combination of the questions below to lead the discussion.

- Explain to your partner how you solved Problem 1(a). Did you have to unbundle a ten or hundred? Did you solve this problem mentally or with a simplifying strategy? How did you check your work?

- What significant differences do you notice about the way you changed your number disks in Problem 1(b) versus 1(c)? How did you show the change using the algorithm?

- For Problem 1(d), use place value language to explain to your partner how your model matches the written subtraction. Compare how you checked your work.

- One student's answer for Problem 1(e), 927 – 628, was 209. What mistake did he make in the written subtraction? How would the chip model have helped him to figure out the correct answer?

- For Problem 2, explain to your partner why the statement is true. Using part–whole language, what do you know about the relationship between addition and subtraction?

Exit Ticket (3 minutes)

After the Student Debrief, instruct students to complete the Exit Ticket. A review of their work will help you assess the students' understanding of the concepts that were presented in the lesson today and plan more effectively for future lessons. You may read the questions aloud to the students.

COMMON CORE™ | Lesson 14: Use math drawings to represent subtraction with up to two decompositions, relate drawings to the algorithm, and use addition to explain why the subtraction method works.
Date: 10/23/13

5.C.20

Name _____ Date _____

1.	10 + 2 =	21.	2 + 9 =
2.	10 + 5 =	22.	4 + 8 =
3.	10 + 1 =	23.	5 + 9 =
4.	8 + 10 =	24.	6 + 6 =
5.	7 + 10 =	25.	7 + 5 =
6.	10 + 3 =	26.	5 + 8 =
7.	12 + 2 =	27.	8 + 3 =
8.	14 + 3 =	28.	6 + 8 =
9.	15 + 4 =	29.	4 + 6 =
10.	17 + 2 =	30.	7 + 6 =
11.	13 + 5 =	31.	7 + 4 =
12.	14 + 4 =	32.	7 + 9 =
13.	16 + 3 =	33.	7 + 7 =
14.	11 + 7 =	34.	8 + 6 =
15.	9 + 2 =	35.	6 + 9 =
16.	9 + 9 =	36.	8 + 5 =
17.	6 + 9 =	37.	4 + 7 =
18.	8 + 9 =	38.	3 + 9 =
19	7 + 8 =	39.	8 + 6 =
20.	8 + 8 =	40.	9 + 4 =

COMMON CORE | Lesson 14: | Use math drawings to represent subtraction with up to two decompositions, relate drawings to the algorithm, and use addition to explain why the subtraction method works. | 5.C.21

Date: | 10/23/13

© 2013 Common Core, Inc. All rights reserved. **commoncore.org**

Name _____   Date _____

1.	$10 + 7 =$	21.	$5 + 8 =$
2.	$9 + 10 =$	22.	$6 + 7 =$
3.	$2 + 10 =$	23.	____ $+ 4 = 12$
4.	$10 + 5 =$	24.	____ $+ 7 = 13$
5.	$11 + 3 =$	25.	$6 +$ ____ $= 14$
6.	$12 + 4 =$	26.	$7 +$ ____ $= 14$
7.	$16 + 3 =$	27.	____ $= 9 + 8$
8.	$15 +$ ____ $= 19$	28.	____ $= 7 + 5$
9.	$18 +$ ____ $= 20$	29.	____ $= 4 + 8$
10.	$13 + 5 =$	30.	$3 + 9 =$
11.	____ $= 4 + 13$	31.	$6 + 7 =$
12.	____ $= 6 + 12$	32.	$8 +$ ____ $= 13$
13.	____ $= 14 + 6$	33.	____ $= 7 + 9$
14.	$9 + 3 =$	34.	$6 + 6 =$
15.	$7 + 9 =$	35.	____ $= 7 + 5$
16.	____ $+ 4 = 11$	36.	____ $= 4 + 8$
17.	____ $+ 6 = 13$	37.	$15 = 7 +$ ____
18.	____ $+ 5 = 12$	38.	$18 =$ ____ $+ 9$
19	$8 + 8 =$	39.	$16 =$ ____ $+ 7$
20.	$6 + 9 =$	40.	$19 = 9 +$ ____

COMMON CORE   Lesson 14:   Use math drawings to represent subtraction with up to two decompositions, relate drawings to the algorithm, and use addition to explain why the subtraction method works.   5.C.22

Date: 10/23/13

Name _____   Date _____

1.	15 - 5 =	21.	15 - 7 =
2.	16 - 6 =	22.	18 - 9 =
3.	17 - 10 =	23.	16 - 8 =
4.	12 - 10 =	24.	15 - 6 =
5.	13 - 3 =	25.	17 - 8 =
6.	11 - 10 =	26.	14 - 6 =
7.	19 - 9 =	27.	16 - 9 =
8.	20 - 10 =	28.	13 - 8 =
9.	14 - 4 =	29.	12 - 5 =
10.	18 - 11 =	30.	11 - 2 =
11.	11 - 2 =	31.	11 - 3 =
12.	12 - 3 =	32.	13 - 8 =
13.	14 - 2 =	33.	16 - 7 =
14.	13 - 4 =	34.	12 - 7 =
15.	11 - 3 =	35.	16 - 3 =
16.	12 - 4 =	36.	19 - 14 =
17.	13 - 2 =	37.	17 - 4 =
18.	14 - 5 =	38.	18 - 16 =
19	11 - 4 =	39.	15 - 11 =
20.	12 - 5 =	40.	20 - 16 =

COMMON CORE™   **Lesson 14:**   Use math drawings to represent subtraction with up to two decompositions, relate drawings to the algorithm, and use addition to explain why the subtraction method works.   **5.C.23**

Date: 10/23/13

Name _____   Date _____

1.	12 - 2 =	21.	13 - 6 =	
2.	15 - 10 =	22.	15 - 9 =	
3.	17 - 11 =	23.	18 - 7 =	
4.	12 - 10 =	24.	14 - 8 =	
5.	18 - 12 =	25.	17 - 9 =	
6.	16 - 13 =	26.	12 – 9 =	
7.	19 - 9 =	27.	13 - 8 =	
8.	20 – 10 =	28.	15 – 7 =	
9.	14 - 12 =	29.	16 - 8 =	
10.	13 - 3 =	30.	14 - 7 =	
11.	_____ = 11 - 2	31.	13 - 9 =	
12.	_____ = 13 - 2	32.	17 - 8 =	
13.	_____ = 12 - 3	33.	16 – 7 =	
14.	_____ = 11 - 4	34.	_____ = 13 - 5	
15.	_____ = 13 - 4	35.	_____ = 15 - 8	
16.	_____ = 14 - 4	36.	_____ = 18 - 9	
17.	_____ = 11 - 3	37.	_____ = 20 - 6	
18.	15 - 6 =	38.	_____ = 20 - 18	
19	16 - 8 =	39.	_____ = 20 - 3	
20.	12 - 5 =	40.	_____ = 20 - 11	

COMMON CORE™   Lesson 14:   Use math drawings to represent subtraction with up to two decompositions, relate drawings to the algorithm, and use addition to explain why the subtraction method works.   **5.C.24**

Date: 10/23/13

Name _____   Date _____

1.	12 + 2 =	21.	13 - 7 =	
2.	14 + 5 =	22.	11 - 8 =	
3.	18 + 2 =	23.	16 – 8 =	
4.	11 + 7 =	24.	12 + 6 =	
5.	9 + 6 =	25.	13 + 2 =	
6.	7 + 8 =	26.	9 + 11 =	
7.	4 + 7 =	27.	6 + 8 =	
8.	13 - 6 =	28.	7 + 9 =	
9.	12 - 8 =	29.	5 + 7 =	
10.	17 - 9 =	30.	13 - 7 =	
11.	14 - 6 =	31.	15 - 8 =	
12.	16 - 7 =	32.	11 – 9 =	
13.	8 + 8 =	33.	12 - 3 =	
14.	7 + 6 =	34.	14 – 5 =	
15.	4 + 9 =	35.	20 - 12 =	
16.	5 + 7 =	36.	8 + 5 =	
17.	6 + 5 =	37.	7 + 4 =	
18.	13 - 8 =	38.	7 + 8 =	
19	16 - 9 =	39.	4 + 9 =	
20.	14 - 8 =	40.	9 + 11 =	

COMMON CORE   Lesson 14:   Use math drawings to represent subtraction with up to two decompositions, relate drawings to the algorithm, and use addition to explain why the subtraction method works.

Date: 10/23/13

Name _____   Date _____

1. Solve by drawing number disks on a chart. Then, use addition to check your work.

a. 469 – 170	Solve vertically or mentally:	Check:
b. 531 - 224	Solve vertically or mentally:	Check:
c. 618 - 229	Solve vertically or mentally:	Check:

Lesson 14:   Use math drawings to represent subtraction with up to two
decompositions, relate drawings to the algorithm, and use addition
to explain why the subtraction method works.

Date: 10/23/13

5.C.26

d. 838 – 384	Solve vertically or mentally:	Check:
e. 927 – 628	Solve vertically or mentally:	Check:

2. If 561 – 387 = 174, then 174 + 387 = 561. Explain why this statement is true using numbers, pictures, or words.

COMMON CORE

Lesson 14:   Use math drawings to represent subtraction with up to two decompositions, relate drawings to the algorithm, and use addition to explain why the subtraction method works.

Date: 10/23/13

5.C.27

Name _____   Date _____

1. Solve by drawing number disks on a chart. Then, use addition to check your work.

a. 375 – 280	Solve vertically or mentally:	Check:
b. 741 - 448	Solve vertically or mentally:	Check:

COMMON CORE™

Lesson 14:

Date:

Use math drawings to represent subtraction with up to two decompositions, relate drawings to the algorithm, and use addition to explain why the subtraction method works.

10/23/13

5.C.28

Name _____   Date _____

1. Solve by drawing number disks on a chart. Then, use addition to check your work.

a. 373 – 180	Solve vertically or mentally:	Check:
b. 463 - 357	Solve vertically or mentally:	Check:
c. 723 - 584	Solve vertically or mentally:	Check:

Lesson 14:   Use math drawings to represent subtraction with up to two decompositions, relate drawings to the algorithm, and use addition to explain why the subtraction method works.

Date: 10/23/13

5.C.29

d. 861 - 673	Solve vertically or mentally	Check
e. 898 - 889	Solve vertically or mentally	Check

2. If 544 + 366 = 910, then 910 – 544 = 366. Explain why this statement is true using numbers, pictures, or words.

COMMON CORE™

Lesson 14: Use math drawings to represent subtraction with up to two decompositions, relate drawings to the algorithm, and use addition to explain why the subtraction method works.

Date: 10/23/13

5.C.30

Lesson 15

Objective: Use math drawings to represent subtraction with up to two decompositions, relate drawings to the algorithm, and use addition to explain why the subtraction method works.

Suggested Lesson Structure

▨ Application Problem	(8 minutes)	
■ Fluency Practice	(12 minutes)	
▨ Concept Development	(30 minutes)	
■ Student Debrief	(10 minutes)	
Total Time	**(60 minutes)**	

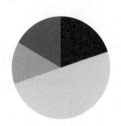

Application Problem (8 minutes)

Catriona earned 16 more stickers than Peter. She earned 35 stickers. How many stickers did Peter earn?

MaryJo earned 47 stickers. How many more does Peter need to have the same amount as MaryJo?

Note: This *compare smaller unknown* problem is intended for guided practice. It is one of the four difficult subtypes of word problems in that the word *more* suggests addition, which would be an incorrect operation. This type of problem highlights the importance of drawing as a way to understand relationships in the problem. The question mark indicates the unknown, as students recognize that they are looking for a missing part.

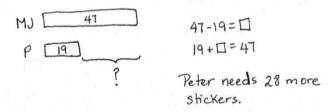

C [35   ]
P [?   ]
          ‿ 16 more

35 − 16 = □
16 + □ = 35
Peter earned 19 stickers.

MJ [47   ]
P [19]
          ⏜ ?

47 − 19 = □
19 + □ = 47
Peter needs 28 more stickers.

Fluency Practice (12 minutes)

- Grade 2 Core Fluency Differentiated Practice Sets **2.OA.2**   (5 minutes)
- Get to 10, 20, or 30 **2.OA.2**   (4 minutes)
- Count by Ten or One with Dimes and Pennies **2.OA.2**   (3 minutes)

COMMON CORE Lesson 15: Use math drawings to present subtraction with up to two decompositions, relate drawings to the algorithm, and use addition to explain why the subtraction method works.

Date: 10/23/13

5.C.31

Grade 2 Core Fluency Differentiated Practice Sets (5 minutes)

Materials: (S) Core Fluency Practice Sets from G2–M5–Lesson 14

Note: During Topic C and for the remainder of the year, each day's fluency includes an opportunity for review and mastery of the sums and differences with totals through 20 by means of the Core Fluency Practice Sets or Sprints. The process is detailed and Practice Sets provided in G2–M5–Lesson 14.

Get to 10, 20, or 30 (4 minutes)

Materials: (S) 3 dimes and 10 pennies

Note: This activity uses dimes and pennies to help students become familiar with coins, while simultaneously providing practice with missing addends to tens.

For the first two minutes:

- Step 1: Lay out 0–10 pennies in 5-group formation and ask students to identify the amount shown (e.g., 9 cents).
- Step 2: Ask for the addition sentence to get to a dime (e.g., 9 cents + 1 cent = 1 dime).

For the next two minutes:

- Repeat Steps 1 and 2, then add a dime and ask students to identify the amount shown (e.g., 1 dime 9 cents + 1 cent = 2 dimes).

Count by Ten or One with Dimes and Pennies (3 minutes)

Materials: (T) 10 dimes and 10 pennies

Note: This activity uses dimes and pennies as abstract representations of tens and ones to help students become familiar with coins, while simultaneously providing practice with counting forward and back by ten or one.

- First minute: Place and take away dimes in a 5-group formation as students count along by ten.
- Second minute: Begin with 2 pennies. Ask how many ones there are. Instruct students to start at 2 and add and subtract 10 as you place and take away dimes.
- Third minute: Begin with 2 dimes. Ask how many tens there are. Instruct students to begin at 20 and add and subtract 1 as you place and take away pennies.

Concept Development (30 minutes)

Materials: (S) Personal white boards, math journals or paper

Note: While this lesson focuses on relating chip models to the subtraction algorithm, guide students towards considering the relationship between the numbers before choosing a strategy to solve.

Lesson 15:	Use math drawings to present subtraction with up to two decompositions, relate drawings to the algorithm, and use addition to explain why the subtraction method works.	5.C.32
Date:	10/23/13	

Problem 1: 430 - 129

T: (Write 430 – 129 horizontally.) Talk with your partner: What do you notice about these numbers?

S: 129 is close to 130, so it's going to be easy to solve mentally. → If you don't even look at the hundreds, you see 30 minus 29. → When I see 129, I think about making the next ten.

T: I like your thinking! So, how would you solve this problem? (Allow students time to solve the problem.)

T: Who can explain their solution?

S: 400 – 100 is 300, and 30 – 29 is 1, so 301. → I used the arrow way and counted on. 129 + 1 is 130, and 130 + 300 is 430, so the answer is 301. → I added 1 to both numbers to make it easier, like 431 – 130. So, 400 – 100 is 300, and 31 – 30 is 1, so 301.

T: I like the way you noticed how close 129 is to 130, and how close 29 is to 30, and the way you used that to help you solve the problem.

T: So, we could solve this mentally, use a simplifying strategy, or use the algorithm. True?

S: True!

T: It's important to think about the numbers before you decide which strategy to use.

> **NOTES ON MULTIPLE MEANS OF ENGAGEMENT:**
>
> Support oral responses by instructing students to write Problem 1 on their personal boards or paper. Since the hundreds may be distracting, have students underline or draw a box around the 30 in 430 and the 29 in 129. This focuses their attention on the nearest ten, and prompts them to notice the opportunity to use a mental math strategy.

Solve 560 - 258 as a guided practice or proceed to Problem 2, depending on the needs of your student.

Problem 2: 941 – 587

T: (Write 941 – 587 horizontally.) How about this one? Mental math or the algorithm?

S: Algorithm!

T: Rewrite the problem with me. (Write the problem vertically as students do the same.)

T: Today let's make our math drawings using the chip model. I'll draw a model on the board while you draw yours. Whisper count as you draw your dots.

S: (Whisper-count and draw.) 100, 200, 300, …941.

T: Use place value language to tell your partner how your model matches the vertical subtraction.

S: I can count my dots: 100, 200, 300, …910, 920, …941. → I put 9 dots in the hundreds place and that's 900, 4 dots in the tens place and that's 40, and 1 dot in the ones place is 1. → My model shows 900 + 40 + 1, that's 941.

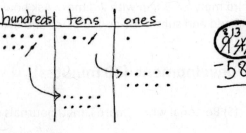

T: Let's draw our magnifying glass and set this problem up to subtract! (Draw a circle around 941 as students do the same.)

T: Look at your model. Are we ready to subtract in the ones?

S: No!

COMMON CORE | Lesson 15: | Use math drawings to present subtraction with up to two decompositions, relate drawings to the algorithm, and use addition to explain why the subtraction method works.

Date: 10/23/13

5.C.33

T: Ask your partner: Where can we get some more ones?

S: From the tens place. → Decompose a ten. → Rename 1 ten as 10 ones.

T: Let's show that on our models. (Cross off 1 ten, draw an arrow to the ones place, and draw 10 ones as students do the same.)

T: How many tens do we have now?

S: 3 tens.

T: Show that with the algorithm. Check your work with mine. (Cross off 4 and write 3 above the tens place as students do the same.)

T: How many ones do you see on the model?

S: 11 ones!

T: Cross off 1 one and write 11 ones. (Record the change as students do the same.)

T: Look at the tens place. Are we ready to subtract in the tens?

S: No!

T: Why not?

S: 4 tens is smaller than 8 tens. → 80 is bigger than 40.

T: Where can we get some more tens? Unbundle a…?

S: Hundred!

T: Let's show that on our models. (Cross off 1 hundred, draw an arrow to the tens place, and draw 10 tens as students do the same.)

T: We need to record the change. How many hundreds do we see now?

S: 8 hundreds!

T: Cross off 9 hundreds and write 8 hundreds. (Record as students do the same.)

T: Look at the tens place on the model. How many tens do we see?

S: 13 tens!

T: Let's record that change as well. (Record as students do the same, changing 3 tens to 13 tens.)

T: Are we completely ready to subtract?

S: Yes! (Allow students time to complete the subtraction.)

T: Talk with your partner. Take turns sharing how you showed the subtraction on your model and using the algorithm. (Allow time for students to share.)

T: I heard some of you notice one of the advantages of getting the problem ready to subtract. You can subtract in any order!

T: Read the complete number sentence.

S: 941 – 587 = 354.

T: How can you prove that this statement is true? If 941 – 587 = 354, then 354 + 587 = 941. Discuss with your partner.

MP.7

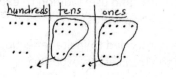

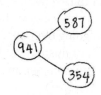

S: You can draw a number bond. → You could do the addition and see if it equals the whole. → If 354 is the missing part, when you add it to the other part, 587, it will equal the whole, 941.

COMMON CORE™

Lesson 15:   Use math drawings to present subtraction with up to two
decompositions, relate drawings to the algorithm, and use addition
to explain why the subtraction method works.

Date: 10/23/13

5.C.34

MP.7

T: Please check the answer by drawing a chip model to add 354 + 587. Check your model and your addition with your partner. If you are correct, write the number bond for this problem.

Circulate to check for understanding and to support struggling students. Project student work or call students to the board to show the chip model, algorithm, and number bond. Encourage students to use place value language to explain their work.

Problem 3: 624 – 225

Follow the above procedure to guide students as they write 624 –225 vertically, model it, and solve. Remind them to be precise in lining up the digits and in drawing their number disks in neat 5-groups. Encourage students to use place value language to explain each action they take on their model and how it is represented using the algorithm. Instruct students to check their work with addition and to explain why this method works.

Repeat the process for 756 – 374 and 817 – 758. Continue to support struggling students, but as they demonstrate proficiency, instruct them to work on the Problem Set independently.

NOTES ON
MULTIPLE MEANS OF
ACTION AND
EXPRESSION:

As students work more independently, adjust the numbers in some problems to suit individual learners' levels:

- For struggling students, choose numbers that will only require one decomposition at a time rather than two.

- For accelerated students, increase the numbers to the thousands to offer a challenge.

Problem Set (10 minutes)

Students should do their personal best to complete the Problem Set within the allotted 10 minutes. For some classes, it may be appropriate to modify the assignment by specifying which problems they work on first. Some problems do not specify a method for solving. Students solve these problems using the RDW approach used for Application Problems.

Student Debrief (10 minutes)

Lesson Objective: Use math drawings to represent subtraction with up to two decompositions, relate drawings to the algorithm, and use addition to explain why the subtraction method works.

The Student Debrief is intended to invite reflection and active processing of the total lesson experience.

Invite students to review their solutions for the Problem Set. They should check work by comparing answers with a partner before going over answers as a class. Look for misconceptions or misunderstandings that can be addressed in the Debrief. Guide students in a conversation to debrief the Problem Set and process the lesson.

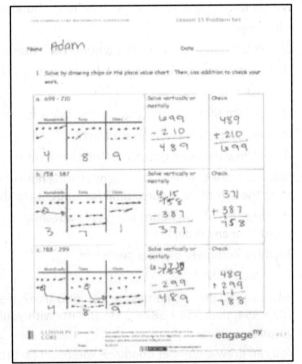

Lesson 15:   Use math drawings to present subtraction with up to two decompositions, relate drawings to the algorithm, and use addition to explain why the subtraction method works.

Date: 10/23/13

5.C.35

You may choose to use any combination of the questions below to lead the discussion.

- For Problem 1(a), which strategy did you use to solve? Why? Why didn't you add one to 699 to make the hundred?

- For Problem 1(b), which strategy did you use to solve? Why? How did you know whether or not to unbundle a ten or hundred? How did you show the change on the written subtraction?

- For Problem 1(c), what is the most efficient way to solve this problem? Why? How was this problem different from Problem 1(a)? How did you check your work?

- For Problem 1(d), what number(s) did you draw on your place value chart? How did you show unbundling with your chips and on the written subtraction?

- For Problem 1(e), how can you tell right away if you will need to decompose a ten or hundred?

- What important math vocabulary have we used to talk about breaking apart a larger unit into smaller units? (*Decompose, rename, unbundle, change.*)

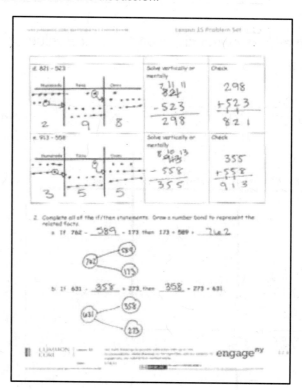

Exit Ticket (3 minutes)

After the Student Debrief, instruct students to complete the Exit Ticket. A review of their work will help you assess the students' understanding of the concepts that were presented in the lesson today and plan more effectively for future lessons. You may read the questions aloud to the students.

Lesson 15: Use math drawings to present subtraction with up to two decompositions, relate drawings to the algorithm, and use addition to explain why the subtraction method works.

Date: 10/23/13

Name _____   Date _____

1. Solve by drawing chips on the place value chart. Then, use addition to check your work.

a. 699 – 210	Solve vertically or mentally:	Check:
Hundreds	Tens	Ones		

b. 758 – 387	Solve vertically or mentally:	Check:
Hundreds	Tens	Ones		

c. 788 – 299	Solve vertically or mentally:	Check:
Hundreds	Tens	Ones		

d. 821 – 523	Solve vertically or mentally:	Check:
Hundreds Tens Ones		

e. 913 – 558	Solve vertically or mentally:	Check:
Hundreds Tens Ones		

2. Complete all of the *if...then* statements. Draw a number bond to represent the related facts.

   a. If 762 – _____ = 173, then 173 + 589 = _____.

   b. If 631 – _____ = 273, then _____ + 273 = 631.

COMMON CORE™

Lesson 15: Use math drawings to present subtraction with up to two decompositions, relate drawings to the algorithm, and use addition to explain why the subtraction method works.

Date: 10/23/13

5.C.38

Name _____ Date _____

Solve by drawing chips on the place value chart. Then, use addition to check your work.

1. 583 – 327	Solve vertically or mentally:	Check:
Hundreds | Tens | Ones		

2. 721 – 485	Solve vertically or mentally:	Check:
Hundreds | Tens | Ones		

COMMON CORE™ **Lesson 15:** Use math drawings to present subtraction with up to two decompositions, relate drawings to the algorithm, and use addition to explain why the subtraction method works. 5.C.39

Date: 10/23/13

© 2013 Common Core, Inc. All rights reserved. commoncore.org

Name _____   Date _____

1. Solve by drawing chips on the place value chart. Then, use addition to check your work.

a. 800 – 675	Solve vertically or mentally:	Check:
Hundreds | Tens | Ones		

b. 742 – 495	Solve vertically or mentally:	Check:
Hundreds | Tens | Ones		

c. 657 – 290	Solve vertically or mentally:	Check:
Hundreds | Tens | Ones		

COMMON CORE™

Lesson 15:   Use math drawings to present subtraction with up to two decompositions, relate drawings to the algorithm, and use addition to explain why the subtraction method works.

Date: 10/23/13

5.C.40

d. 877 – 398	Solve vertically or mentally:	Check:
Hundreds | Tens | Ones		

e. 941 – 628	Solve vertically or mentally:	Check:
Hundreds | Tens | Ones		

2. Complete all of the *if…then* statements. Draw a number bond to represent the related facts.

   a. If **928 – _____ = 519**, then **519 + 409 = _____**.

   b. If **764 – _____ = 391**, then **_____ + 391 = 764**.

Lesson 16

Objective: Subtract from multiples of 100 and from numbers with zero in the tens place.

Suggested Lesson Structure

■ Application Problem   (8 minutes)
■ Fluency Practice   (12 minutes)
□ Concept Development   (30 minutes)
■ Student Debrief   (10 minutes)

  Total Time   **(60 minutes)**

Application Problem (8 minutes)

Will read 15 more pages than Marcy. Marcy read 38 pages. The book is 82 pages long.

   a)   How many pages did Will read?

   b)   How many more pages does Will need to read to finish the book?

Note: This two-step problem is intended for guided practice, as students gain familiarity with the *compare bigger unknown* problem type. Tape diagrams enable students to make sense of the relationships between the numbers and to effectively choose an operation to both represent the situation and to solve.

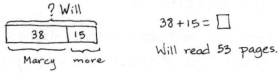

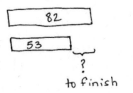

$38 + 15 = \square$

Will read 53 pages.

$82 - 53 = \square$

$53 + \square = 82$

Will needs to read 29 more pages.

Fluency Practice (12 minutes)

▪ Sprint: Subtraction from Teens **2.OA.2**   (8 minutes)
▪ Coin Drop **2.OA.2**   (2 minutes)
▪ More and Less **2.NBT.5**   (2 minutes)

Sprint: Subtraction from Teens (8 minutes)

Materials: (S) Subtraction from Teens Sprint

Note: Students practice subtraction from teens in order to gain mastery of the sums and differences within 20.

Lesson 16: Subtract from multiples of 100 and from numbers with zero in the tens place.

Date: 10/23/13

5.C.42

Coin Drop (2 minutes)

Materials: (T) 10 dimes, 10 pennies, can

Note: In this activity, students practice adding and subtracting ones and tens using coins, in preparation for Module 7.

 T: (Hold up a penny.) Name my coin.
 S: A penny.
 T: How much is it worth?
 S: 1 cent.
 T: Listen carefully as I drop coins in my can. Count along in your minds.

Drop in some pennies and ask how much money is in the can. Take out some pennies and show them. Ask how much money is still in the can. Continue adding and subtracting pennies for a minute or so. Then repeat the activity with dimes, then with dimes and pennies.

More and Less (2 minutes)

Materials: (T) 10 dimes, 10 pennies

Note: In this activity, students practice adding and subtracting ones and tens using coins.

 T: Let's count by tens. (Move dimes to the side while counting.)
 S: 10, 20, 30, 40, 50, 60.
 T: How many dimes are shown?
 S: 6 dimes.
 T: What is the value of 6 dimes?
 S: 60 cents.
 T: What is 5 cents more? (Move 5 pennies.)
 S: 65 cents.
 T: Give the number sentence.
 S: 60 cents + 5 cents = 65 cents.
 T: What is 10 cents less? (Move 1 dime.)
 S: 55 cents.
 T: Give the number sentence.
 S: 65 cents − 10 cents = 55 cents.

Continue to repeat this line of questioning with a similar sequence of numbers.

Concept Development (30 minutes)

Materials: (S) Personal white boards, math journals or paper

Lesson 16: Subtract from multiples of 100 and from numbers with zero in the tens place.
Date: 10/23/13

5.C.43

Note: This Concept Development extends student learning from G2–M4–Lessons 27–28.

Problem 1: 402 - 231

T: (Write 402 – 231 horizontally.) Let's solve this problem using a math drawing and the algorithm.

T: Rewrite the problem with me. (Write the problem vertically as students do the same.)

T: Which number is the whole?

S: 402!

T: Let's make a chip model to show the whole. I'll draw it on the board while you draw yours. Whisper-count as you draw your dots.

S: (Whisper-count and draw.) 100, 200, 300, 400, 401, 402.

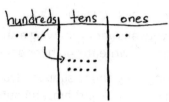 

T: Let's draw our magnifying glass and get ready to subtract! (Draw a circle around 402 as students do the same.)

T: Look at your model. Are we ready to subtract in the ones?

S: Yes!

T: Moving on, let's look at the tens place. I don't see any tens in the tens place on the model. Point to the digit that represents this in the algorithm.

S: (Point to the 0.)

T: The zero holds the tens place open and tells us the number is 402.

T: Without that 0, what number would we read? (Write 42.)

S: 42!

T: (Erase 42.) Yes, so we must be precise when writing and representing numbers.

T: Where can we get some tens so we can subtract 3 tens?

S: The hundreds place. → Decompose a hundred. → Rename 1 hundred as 10 tens.

T: Let's show that on our models. Count with me as we rename 1 hundred as 10 tens. (Cross off 1 hundred, draw an arrow to the tens place, and draw 10 dots, or tens.)

S: (Draw and count.) 10, 20, 30, 40, 50, 60, 70, 80, 90, 100!

T: Show that using the algorithm. As I do the same, check your work with mine. (Cross off 4 and write 3 above the hundreds place, then cross off 0 and write 10 above the tens place. Students do the same.)

T: Are we ready to subtract now in the tens place?

S: Yes!

T: Let's look at the hundreds place. Are we ready to subtract in the hundreds?

NOTES ON
MULTIPLE MEANS OF
ENGAGEMENT:

It is easy to lose students when subtraction involves zeros in the minuend. Check frequently for understanding by establishing a quiet, non-verbal signal (e.g., thumbs-up) that students can use to indicate whether or not they are following.

Lesson 16:   Subtract from multiples of 100 and from numbers with zero in the tens place.

Date: 10/23/13

5.C.44

S: Yes!

T: Then we're ready to subtract! (Allow students time to complete the subtraction.)

T: Talk with your partner. Take turns sharing how you showed the subtraction on your model and using the algorithm. (Allow students time to share.)

T: Read the complete number sentence.

S: $402 - 231 = 171$.

T: How can we prove that our answer is correct?

S: Add the parts to see if they equal the whole.

T: Yes! Please check your answer by drawing a chip model to add the two parts. If you are correct, write the number bond for this problem.

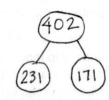

Circulate to check for understanding and to support struggling students. Project student work or call students to the board to show the chip model, algorithm, and number bond. Encourage students to use place value language to explain their work.

Problem 2: 800 − 463

Follow the above procedure to guide students as they write $800 - 463$ vertically and model it.

T: Talk with your partner. What do you notice about the whole and what will we need to do?

S: This time there are no tens and no ones. → We need to unbundle a hundred to make tens *and* ones. → We need to rename 1 hundred as 9 tens 10 ones.

T: Let's do that. Count aloud as you rename 1 hundred as 9 tens 10 ones. (Cross off 1 hundred, draw an arrow to the tens place, and draw 9 tens as students do the same.)

MP.8

S: 10, 20, 30, 40, 50, 60, 70, 80, 90.

T: Stop! Now, count on as you draw the ones. (Draw 10 ones as students do the same.)

S: 91, 92, 93, 94, 95, 96, 97, 98, 99, 100.

T: So 1 hundred is the same as 9 tens 10 ones. True?

S: True!

> **NOTES ON MULTIPLE MEANS OF REPRESENTATION:**
>
> While some students prefer to rename 800 in one step (e.g. 7 hundreds, 9 tens, 10 ones), others may need the intermediate step of renaming a hundred as 10 tens before renaming a ten as 10 ones. Allow students to use number disks or chips to model the decomposition in two steps.

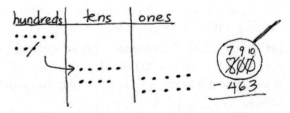

Continue using the procedure from Problem 1 to guide students as they complete the subtraction on both the model and the algorithm, share their work, and verify their solution to Problem 2 using addition.

Repeat the process for $908 - 120$, $705 - 36$, $600 - 316$, and $500 - 327$. Continue to support struggling students, but as they demonstrate proficiency, instruct them to work on the Problem Set independently.

Lesson 16: Subtract from multiples of 100 and from numbers with zero in the tens place.

Date: 10/23/13

5.C.45

Problem Set (10 minutes)

Students should do their personal best to complete the Problem Set within the allotted 10 minutes. For some classes, it may be appropriate to modify the assignment by specifying which problems they work on first. Some problems do not specify a method for solving. Students solve these problems using the RDW approach used for Application Problems.

Student Debrief (10 minutes)

Lesson Objective: Subtract from multiples of 100 and from numbers with zero in the tens place.

The Student Debrief is intended to invite reflection and active processing of the total lesson experience.

Invite students to review their solutions for the Problem Set. They should check work by comparing answers with a partner before going over answers as a class. Look for misconceptions or misunderstandings that can be addressed in the Debrief. Guide students in a conversation to debrief the Problem Set and process the lesson.

You may choose to use any combination of the questions below to lead the discussion.

- For Problem 1(a), 304 – 53, explain how you solved this problem. How could you have solved it mentally?

- For Problem 1(b), 406 – 187, what did you draw on your place value chart? How did you unbundle 400? Did you do it in one or two steps?

- For Problem 1(c), 501 – 316, explain to your partner how you changed a larger unit to make more ones when there were no tens?

- For Problem 1(d), what are two different ways you can unbundle 700? How can you do it in one step? How could you have solved this problem mentally?

- Think like a detective: When you are subtracting three-digit numbers, when do you choose to unbundle a hundred? When do you choose to solve mentally? What clues in the numbers help you to choose a solution strategy?

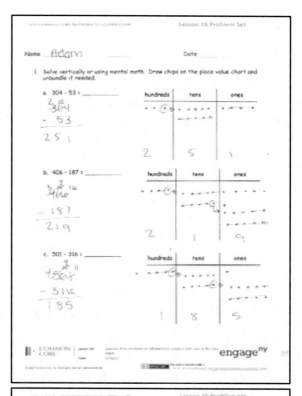

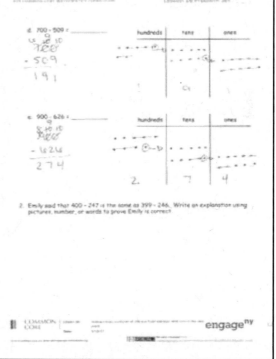

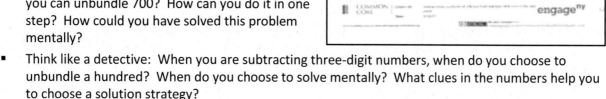

Lesson 16:   Subtract from multiples of 100 and from numbers with zero in the tens place.
Date: 10/23/13

5.C.46

Exit Ticket (3 minutes)

After the Student Debrief, instruct students to complete the Exit Ticket. A review of their work will help you assess the students' understanding of the concepts that were presented in the lesson today and plan more effectively for future lessons. You may read the questions aloud to the students.

Lesson 16:   Subtract from multiples of 100 and from numbers with zero in the tens place.
Date: 10/23/13

5.C.47

A

Correct _____

Subtract.

1	11 - 10 =		23	19 - 9 =	
2	12 - 10 =		24	15 - 6 =	
3	13 - 10 =		25	15 - 7 =	
4	19 - 10 =		26	15 - 9 =	
5	11 - 1 =		27	20 - 10 =	
6	12 - 2 =		28	14 - 5 =	
7	13 - 3 =		29	14 - 6 =	
8	17 - 7 =		30	14 - 7 =	
9	11 - 2 =		31	14 - 9 =	
10	11 - 3 =		32	15 - 5 =	
11	11 - 4 =		33	17 - 8 =	
12	11 - 8 =		34	17 - 9 =	
13	18 - 8 =		35	18 - 8 =	
14	13 - 4 =		36	16 - 7 =	
15	13 - 5 =		37	16 - 8 =	
16	13 - 6 =		38	16 - 9 =	
17	13 - 8 =		39	17 - 10 =	
18	16 - 6 =		40	12 - 8 =	
19	12 - 3 =		41	18 - 9 =	
20	12 - 4 =		42	11 - 9 =	
21	12 - 5 =		43	15 - 8 =	
22	12 - 9 =		44	13 - 7 =	

© Bill Davidson

COMMON CORE™

Lesson 16: Subtract from multiples of 100 and from numbers with zero in the tens place.

Date: 10/23/13

5.C.48

B

Improvement _____   # Correct _____

Subtract.

1	11 - 1 =		23	16 - 6 =	
2	12 - 2 =		24	14 - 5 =	
3	13 - 3 =		25	14 - 6 =	
4	18 - 8 =		26	14 - 7 =	
5	11 - 10 =		27	14 - 9 =	
6	12 - 10 =		28	20 - 10 =	
7	13 - 10 =		29	15 - 6 =	
8	18 - 10 =		30	15 - 7 =	
9	11 - 2 =		31	15 - 9 =	
10	11 - 3 =		32	14 - 4 =	
11	11 - 4 =		33	16 - 7 =	
12	11 - 7 =		34	16 - 8 =	
13	19 - 9 =		35	16 - 9 =	
14	12 - 3 =		36	20 - 10 =	
15	12 - 4 =		37	17 - 8 =	
16	12 - 5 =		38	17 - 9 =	
17	12 - 8 =		39	16 - 10 =	
18	17 - 7 =		40	18 - 9 =	
19	13 - 4 =		41	12 - 9 =	
20	13 - 5 =		42	13 - 7 =	
21	13 - 6 =		43	11 - 8 =	
22	13 - 9 =		44	15 - 8 =	

© Bill Davidson

COMMON CORE™   **Lesson 16:**   Subtract from multiples of 100 and from numbers with zero in the tens place.

Date: 10/23/13

5.C.49

Name _____   Date _____

1. Solve vertically or using mental math. Draw chips on the place value chart and unbundle if needed.

    a. 304 – 53 = _____

hundreds	tens	ones

    b. 406 – 187 = _____

hundreds	tens	ones

    c. 501 – 316 = _____

hundreds	tens	ones

d. 700 – 509 = _____

hundreds	tens	ones

e. 900 – 626 = _____

hundreds	tens	ones

2. Emily said that 400 – 247 is the same as 399 – 246. Write an explanation using pictures, number, or words to prove Emily is correct.

Name _____   Date _____

1. Solve vertically or using mental math. Draw chips on the place value chart and unbundle if needed.

a. 604 – 143 = _____

hundreds	tens	ones

b. 700 – 568 = _____

hundreds	tens	ones

COMMON CORE™   Lesson 16:   Subtract from multiples of 100 and from numbers with zero in the tens place.

Date: 10/23/13

5.C.52

Name _____   Date _____

1. Solve vertically or using mental math. Draw chips on the place value chart and unbundle if needed.

   a. 206 – 89 = _____

hundreds	tens	ones

   b. 509 – 371 = _____

hundreds	tens	ones

   c. 607 – 288 = _____

hundreds	tens	ones

5.C.54

d. 800 – 608 = _____

hundreds	tens	ones

e. 900 – 572 = _____

hundreds	tens	ones

2. Andy said that 599 – 456 is the same as 600 – 457. Write an explanation using pictures, number, or words to prove Andy is correct.

COMMON CORE™

Lesson 16:   Subtract from multiples of 100 and from numbers with zero in the tens place.

Date: 10/23/13

5.C.54

Lesson 17

Objective: Subtract from multiples of 100 and from numbers with zero in the tens place.

Suggested Lesson Structure

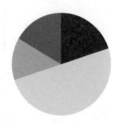

■ Application Problem	(8 minutes)
■ Fluency Practice	(12 minutes)
■ Concept Development	(30 minutes)
■ Student Debrief	(10 minutes)
Total Time	**(60 minutes)**

Application Problem (8 minutes)

Colleen put 27 fewer beads on her necklace than Jenny did. Colleen put on 46 beads. How many beads did Jenny put on her necklace?

If 16 beads fell off of Jenny's necklace, how many beads are still on it?

Note: This *compare bigger unknown* problem is intended for guided practice. It is one of the four difficult subtypes of word problems in that the word *fewer* suggests subtraction, which would be an incorrect operation.

This type of problem highlights the importance of drawing as a way to understand the relationship between numbers in the problem. The question mark indicates the unknown, as students recognize that they are looking for the whole or a missing part.

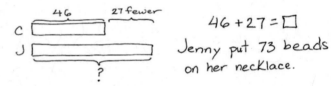

$46 + 27 = \Box$

Jenny put 73 beads on her necklace.

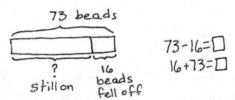

$73 - 16 = \Box$

$16 + 73 = \Box$

57 beads are still on Jenny's necklace.

Fluency Practice (12 minutes)

- Sprint: Subtract Crossing the Ten **2.OA.2, 2.NBT.5**   (8 minutes)
- Using the Nearest Ten to Subtract **2.NBT.5**   (2 minutes)
- Subtract Common Units **2.NBT.5, 2.NBT.7**   (2 minutes)

Sprint: Subtract Crossing the Ten (8 minutes)

Materials: (S) Subtract Crossing the Ten Sprint

Lesson 17:	Subtract from multiples of 100 and from numbers with zero in the tens place.	
Date:	10/23/13	

5.C.55

Note: Students practice subtracting crossing the ten in preparation for the lesson and to gain mastery of the sums and differences within 20.

Using the Nearest Ten to Subtract (2 minutes)

Note: Reviewing the Grade 1 skill of counting up and down to 10 to subtract gives students a mental strategy to subtract fluently with larger numbers.

T: (Write 16 – 9 on the board.) Raise your hand when you know the answer to 16 – 9.
S: 7.
T: (Write in the bond.) 10 – 9 is ___?
S: 1.
T: 1 + 6 is...?
S: 7.

Continue with the following possible sequence: 15 – 9, 13 – 8, 15 – 7, 16 – 7, 12 – 9, 13 – 7, 23 – 7, 25 – 7, 25 – 9, 26 – 9, 27 – 9, 27 – 9, 37 – 9, 37 – 19, 35 – 19, 45 – 19, 47 – 18, 48 – 29.

Subtract Common Units (2 minutes)

Note: Reviewing this mental math fluency prepares students for understanding the importance of the subtraction algorithm and place value.

T: (Project 77.) Say the number in unit form.
S: 7 tens 7 ones.
T: (Write 77 – 22 = ____.) Say the subtraction sentence and answer in unit form.
S: 7 tens 7 ones – 2 tens 2 ones = 5 tens 5 ones.
T: Write the subtraction sentence on your boards.

Continue with the following possible sequence: 88 – 33, 66 – 44, 266 – 44, 55 – 33, and 555 – 33.

Concept Development (30 minutes)

Materials: (S) Personal white boards, math journals or paper

Note: This lesson is a continuation of G2–M5–Lesson 16; it extends the student learning from G2–M4–Lessons 27–28.

Problem 1: 300 - 195

T: (Write 300 – 195 horizontally.) Talk with your partner: What do you notice about these numbers?
S: 195 is close to 200, so it's going to be easy to solve mentally. → If you add 5 to 195 it will be 200, which makes it easy to subtract from 300. → Yeah, making a hundred is just like making a ten.
T: Excellent reasoning! It's a good math habit to think about the numbers and how they relate to each other before you decide on a strategy.

Lesson 17:   Subtract from multiples of 100 and from numbers with zero in the
tens place.
Date: 10/23/13

5.C.56

T: Take a moment to solve this problem using the strategy you like best, and be prepared to explain why it works.

T: Who can explain their solution?

S: I thought about this as an addition problem starting with 195. I used arrow notation and wrote 195 + 5 is 200, and 200 + 100 is 300, so 100 + 5 is 105. → I broke 300 into 100 and 200, and I subtracted 195 from 200. That left 100 and 5, which is 105. → 305 − 200 is 105, I added 5 to 195 and 5 to 300. The difference stays the same, 105.

T: So we could solve this mentally, use a simplifying strategy, or use the algorithm. True?

S: True!

T: Keep that in mind, even as we use models and the algorithm to solve some more problems.

Problem 2: 500 − 213

T: (Write 500 − 213 horizontally.) Let's set this problem up to solve using the chip model and the algorithm.

T: Rewrite the problem with me. (Write the problem vertically as students do the same.)

T: Let's make a chip model to show the whole. I'll draw it on the board while you draw yours. Whisper-count as you draw your dots.

S: (Whisper-count and draw.) 100, 200, 300, 400, 500.

T: Now, draw the magnifying glass. (Draw a circle around 500 as students do the same.)

T: Are we ready to subtract?

S: No.

T: Tell your partner what we need to do.

S: There are no tens and ones, so we have to open up a hundred. → We need to rename 1 hundred as 10 tens. Then, cross out 1 ten and rename it as 10 ones. → We need to change 1 hundred for 9 tens 10 ones.

T: Let's do that. Count aloud as you rename 1 hundred as 9 tens 10 ones. (Cross off 1 hundred, draw an arrow to the tens place, and draw 9 tens as students do the same.)

MP.8

S: (Draw and count.) 10, 20, 30, 40, 50, 60, 70, 80, 90.

T: Count on as you draw the ones. (Draw 10 ones as students do the same.)

S: (Draw and count.) 91, 92, 93, 94, 95, 96, 97, 98, 99, 100.

T: Look at your model. What number is 9 tens?

S: 90!

T: And 10 ones?

NOTES ON MULTIPLE MEANS OF ENGAGEMENT:

Although students work extensively with the algorithm in these modules, they will not be assessed on the algorithm until Grade 3. When students build a solid conceptual understanding of subtraction at this level, fluency and accuracy with the algorithm should increase greatly.

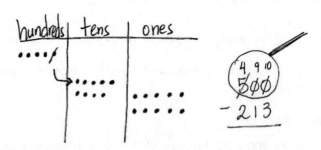

COMMON CORE™

Lesson 17:   Subtract from multiples of 100 and from numbers with zero in the tens place.

Date: 10/23/13

5.C.57

S: 10!

T: 90 + 10 = ?

S: 100!

T: So we can rename 1 hundred as 9 tens 10 ones. True?

S: True!

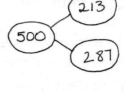

MP.8 T: Now we need to show these changes using the algorithm. As I record the changes on the numbers, check your work with mine. (Cross off 5 and write 4 above the hundreds place. Cross off 0 tens and write 9 above the tens place, then cross off 0 ones and write 10 above the ones place.)

T: Complete the subtraction, then take turns sharing how your work on the model matches the steps of the algorithm. (Allow students time to share.)

T: Read the complete number sentence.

S: 500 – 213 = 287.

T: How can we prove that our answer is correct?

S: Add the parts to see if they equal the whole.

T: Correct! Please check your answer by drawing a chip model to add the two parts. If you are correct, write the number bond for this problem.

Circulate to check for understanding and to support struggling students. Project student work or call students to the board to show the chip model, algorithm, and number bond. Encourage students to use place value language to explain their work.

NOTES ON MULTIPLE MEANS OF EXPRESSION:

For students who may be impatient to use the algorithm alone, encourage them to use the models to show their thinking. Explain that while the student may know what she is doing, others who look at her work are helped by seeing the work written out. Models are also helpful for checking work.

Problem 3: 603 – 487

Follow the above procedure to guide students as they write 603 – 487 vertically, model it, and solve. Remind them to be precise in lining up the digits and in drawing their dots in neat 5-groups. Encourage students to use place value language to explain each action that they take on their model and how it is represented using the algorithm. Instruct students to check their work with addition and to explain why this method works.

Repeat the process for 801 – 634 and 900 – 576 or move on to the Problem Set. Continue to support struggling students, but as they demonstrate proficiency, instruct them to work on the Problem Set independently.

Problem Set (10 minutes)

Students should do their personal best to complete the Problem Set within the allotted 10 minutes. For some classes, it may be appropriate to modify the assignment by specifying which problems they work on first. Some problems do not specify a method for solving. Students solve these problems using the RDW approach used for Application Problems.

Lesson 17: Subtract from multiples of 100 and from numbers with zero in the tens place.

Date: 10/23/13

5.C.58

© 2013 Common Core, Inc. All rights reserved. **commoncore.org**

Student Debrief (10 minutes)

Lesson Objective: Subtract from multiples of 100 and from numbers with zero in the tens place.

The Student Debrief is intended to invite reflection and active processing of the total lesson experience.

Invite students to review their solutions for the Problem Set. They should check work by comparing answers with a partner before going over answers as a class. Look for misconceptions or misunderstandings that can be addressed in the Debrief. Guide students in a conversation to debrief the Problem Set and process the lesson.

You may choose to use any combination of the questions below to lead the discussion.

- For Problem 1, which problems did you choose to solve mentally? Why? What made some easier than others?

- For Problem 1(b), how did you rename 400 using your chips? Show me what 400 looks like after you have renamed the units.

- Explain to your partner the steps you took to set up Problem 1(c). How was this similar to 1(b)?

- Trey solved Problem 1(d), 800 − 606, by using place value, 800 − 600 = 200. Then he added 6 more, since one part was 606, so the answer was 206. What was his error?

- For Problem 1(d), explain the meaning of the 9 in the tens place.

Exit Ticket (3 minutes)

After the Student Debrief, instruct students to complete the Exit Ticket. A review of their work will help you assess the students' understanding of the concepts that were presented in the lesson today and plan more effectively for future lessons. You may read the questions aloud to the students.

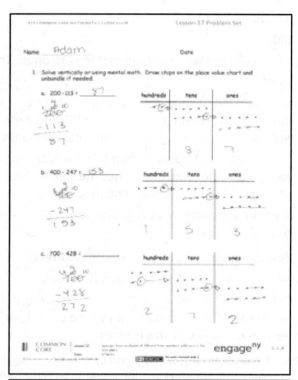

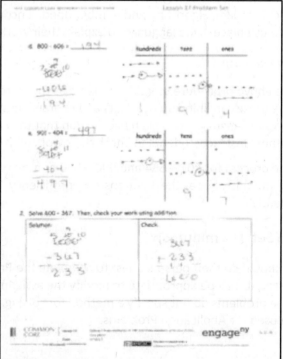

COMMON CORE

Lesson 17:   Subtract from multiples of 100 and from numbers with zero in the tens place.
Date: 10/23/13

5.C.59

A

Subtract.

Correct _____

1	10 - 1 =		23	21 - 6 =	
2	10 - 2 =		24	91 - 6 =	
3	20 - 2 =		25	10 - 7 =	
4	40 - 2 =		26	11 - 7 =	
5	10 - 2 =		27	31 - 7 =	
6	11 - 2 =		28	10 - 8 =	
7	21 - 2 =		29	11 - 8 =	
8	51 - 2=		30	41 - 8 =	
9	10 - 3 =		31	10 - 9 =	
10	11 - 3 =		32	11 - 9 =	
11	21 - 3 =		33	51 - 9 =	
12	61 - 3 =		34	12 - 3 =	
13	10 - 4 =		35	82 - 3 =	
14	11 - 4 =		36	13 - 5 =	
15	21 - 4 =		37	73 - 5 =	
16	71 - 4 =		38	14 - 6 =	
17	10 - 5 =		39	84 - 6 =	
18	11 - 5 =		40	15 - 8 =	
19	21 - 5 =		41	95 - 8 =	
20	81 - 5 =		42	16 - 7 =	
21	10 - 6 =		43	46 - 7 =	
22	11 - 6 =		44	68 - 9 =	

© Bill Davidson

98

 Lesson 17: Subtract from multiples of 100 and from numbers with zero in the tens place.

Date: 10/23/13

5.C.60

B

Improvement _____   # Correct _____

Subtract.

1	10 - 2 =		23	21 - 6 =	
2	20 - 2 =		24	41 - 6 =	
3	30 - 2 =		25	10 - 7 =	
4	50 - 2 =		26	11 - 7 =	
5	10 - 2 =		27	51 - 7 =	
6	11 - 2 =		28	10 - 8 =	
7	21 - 2 =		29	11 - 8 =	
8	61 - 2 =		30	61 - 8 =	
9	10 - 3 =		31	10 - 9 =	
10	11 - 3 =		32	11 - 9 =	
11	21 - 3 =		33	31 - 9 =	
12	71 - 3 =		34	12 - 3 =	
13	10 - 4 =		35	92 - 3 =	
14	11 - 4 =		36	13 - 5 =	
15	21 - 4 =		37	43 - 5 =	
16	81 - 4 =		38	14 - 6 =	
17	10 - 5 =		39	64 - 6 =	
18	11 - 5 =		40	15 - 8 =	
19	21 - 5 =		41	85 - 8 =	
20	91 - 5 =		42	16 - 7 =	
21	10 - 6 =		43	76 - 7 =	
22	11 - 6 =		44	58 - 9 =	

© Bill Davidson

100

COMMON CORE | Lesson 17: | Subtract from multiples of 100 and from numbers with zero in the tens place.
                                   | **Date:** | 10/23/13

5.C.61

Name _____   Date _____

1. Solve vertically or using mental math. Draw chips on the place value chart and unbundle if needed.

a. 200 – 113 = _____

hundreds	tens	ones

b. 400 – 247 = _____

hundreds	tens	ones

c. 700 – 428 = _____

hundreds	tens	ones

Lesson 17:   Subtract from multiples of 100 and from numbers with zero in the tens place.

Date: 10/23/13

5.C.62

© 2013 Common Core, Inc. All rights reserved. **commoncore.org**

d. 800 – 606 = _____

hundreds	tens	ones

e. 901 – 404 = _____

hundreds	tens	ones

2. Solve 600 – 367. Then, check your work using addition.

Solution:	Check:

COMMON CORE

Lesson 17:   Subtract from multiples of 100 and from numbers with zero in the
             tens place.

Date: 10/23/13

© 2013 Common Core, Inc. All rights reserved. commoncore.org

5.C.63

Name _____   Date _____

Solve vertically or using mental math. Draw chips on the place value chart and unbundle if needed.

1. 600 – 432 = _____

hundreds	tens	ones

2. . 303 – 254 = _____

hundreds	tens	ones

COMMON CORE™   **Lesson 17:**   Subtract from multiples of 100 and from numbers with zero in the
                              tens place.
               Date: 10/23/13

© 2013 Common Core, Inc. All rights reserved. **commoncore.org**

5.C.64

Name _____   Date _____

1. Solve vertically or using mental math. Draw chips on the place value chart and unbundle if needed.

a. 200 – 123 = _____

hundreds	tens	ones

b. 400 – 219 = _____

hundreds	tens	ones

c. 700 – 542 = _____

hundreds	tens	ones

COMMON CORE™

Lesson 17:   Subtract from multiples of 100 and from numbers with zero in the tens place.
Date: 10/23/13

5.C.65

d. 800 – 409 = _____

hundreds	tens	ones

e. 905 – 606 = _____

hundreds	tens	ones

2. Solve 800 – 567. Then, check your work using addition.

Solution:	Check:

COMMON CORE™

Lesson 17:   Subtract from multiples of 100 and from numbers with zero in the tens place.
Date: 10/23/13

5.C.66

Lesson 18

Objective: Apply and explain alternate methods for subtracting from multiples of 100 and from numbers with zero in the tens place.

Suggested Lesson Structure

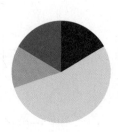

■ Fluency Practice   (10 minutes)
■ Application Problem   (8 minutes)
□ Concept Development   (32 minutes)
■ Student Debrief   (10 minutes)
    Total Time   **(60 minutes)**

Fluency Practice (10 minutes)

- Grade 2 Core Fluency Differentiated Practice Sets **2.OA.2**   (5 minutes)
- Get the Ten Out and Subtract **2.NBT.5**   (5 minutes)

Grade 2 Core Fluency Differentiated Practice Sets (5 minutes)

Materials: (S) Core Fluency Practice Sets

Note: During Topic C and for the remainder of the year, each day's fluency includes an opportunity for review and mastery of the sums and differences with totals through 20 by means of the Core Fluency Practice Sets or Sprints.

Get the Ten Out and Subtract (5 minutes)

Note: Students practice taking out the ten and subtracting to prepare for unbundling a ten in today's lesson.

   T: For every number sentence I give, subtract the ones from ten. When I say $12 - 4$, you say $10 - 4 = 6$. Ready?

   T: $12 - 4$.

   S: $10 - 4 = 6$.

   T: $13 - 7$.

   S: $10 - 7 = 3$.

Practice taking the ten out of number sentences fluently before adding the ones back.

   T: Now let's add back the ones.

   T: $12 - 4$. Take from ten.

Lesson 18:   Apply and explain alternate methods for subtracting from multiples of
100 and from numbers with zero in the tens place.
Date: 10/23/13

5.C.67

S: 10 − 4 = 6.

T: Now add back the ones.

S: 6 + 2 = 8.

Continue with the following possible sequence: 13 − 7, 11 − 8, 13 − 9, 15 − 7, 14 − 8.

Application Problem (8 minutes)

Joseph collected 49 golf balls from the course. He still had 38 fewer than his friend Ethan. How many balls did Ethan have?

If Ethan gave Joseph 24 golf balls, who had more golf balls? How many more?

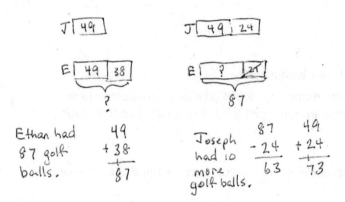

NOTES ON
MULTIPLE MEANS OF
ACTION
AND EXPRESSION:

Initially adjust numbers in the calculation so that students can see that you need to add, rather than subtract, as the word *fewer* suggests.

For example, replace the two-digit numbers with single-digit numbers to emphasize the relationships. For example, Joseph collected six golf balls from the course. He still had three fewer than his friend. With smaller, more manageable numbers, students can use one-to-one matching to make sense of this comparison problem-type.

Use concrete materials to model the second part for students who still struggle to grasp the concept.

Note: In addition to the *compare bigger unknown* component of G2–M5–Lesson 17's Application Problem, this problem requires students to shift quantities from one boy to the other (24 from Joseph to Ethan) and then to find the difference. In this case, drawing a tape diagram highlights the shifting quantities and enables the students to visualize the more complex processes. Lead students in the RDW process, or encourage them to work together to solve and check their work.

Concept Development (32 minutes)

Materials: (S) Personal white boards

Problem 1: Use compensation to solve 300 − 159.

T: (Write 300 − 159 on the board.) We know we can use the vertical method to subtract from the hundred. Is this something we can do quickly?

Lesson 18:   Apply and explain alternate methods for subtracting from multiples of
                100 and from numbers with zero in the tens place.
Date: 10/23/13

5.C.68

S: No, because we have to decompose numbers. → No, we have to unbundle twice to subtract.

T: I'm going to show you a really cool way to make this easier to subtract.

T: (Draw the tape diagram at right on the board.) What happens if I take one off each number? What is my new subtraction problem?

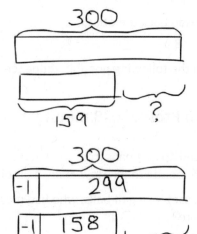

S: 299 – 158.

T: (Draw new tape diagram showing the compensation.)

T: Is this any easier to solve? Turn and talk with a partner.

S: Yes! There's no renaming. → Now we're ready to subtract in all place values!

T: Solve this problem and turn your board over when you are finished.

T: What is 299 – 158?

S: 141!

T: Is this similar to a strategy you've used before? Talk with a partner.

S: It's like when we added the same number to both numbers. → Yes, like with those other tape diagrams where they both got bigger by the same amount. → I think it was called *compensation*.

Problem 2: Add to solve 400 – 278.

T: (Write 400 – 278 on the board.) Let's try a different way to subtract from the hundred. Can we use a different operation to solve?

S: Yes, we can start with 278 and count up to 400. → We can start with 278, which is one part, and use the arrow way to show the other part. → 400 minus 278 is like 278 plus something equals 400.

T: (Draw a number bond with these numbers on the board.)

T: (Write 278 + ____ = 400.) Why can I write the problem like this? Talk with a partner.

S: Because 400 is the whole, and we know one part. → Part plus part makes whole. We don't know one of the parts, so we make it a blank.

T: Let's use the arrow way to solve this problem. (Write 278 → on the board.) How many more do we need to make the next ten?

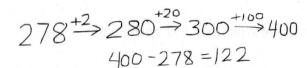

$$278 \xrightarrow{+2} 280 \xrightarrow{+20} 300 \xrightarrow{+100} 400$$
$$400 - 278 = 122$$

S: 2!

T: (Write 2 above the arrow, then 280.)

T: How many more do we need now to get to the next hundred? (Record student responses.)

S: 20! → 2 tens.

T: How many more do we need to get to our whole?

S: 100!

Lesson 18:   Apply and explain alternate methods for subtracting from multiples of
               100 and from numbers with zero in the tens place.
Date: 10/23/13

5.C.69

T: We wrote 2, then 20, then 100. Put them all together, and what do we get?

S: 122!

T: So 400 − 278 is?

S: 122!

Problem 3: 605 − 498

T: Now, let's subtract from a number with a zero in the tens place. Which strategies could we use to solve this problem?

S: We could use the arrow way to solve it with addition, because it's easy to make 500 and then get to 605. → We could take 6 off both numbers to make 599 − 492, which means we don't have to do any renaming. → We could just use the algorithm.

NOTES ON MULTIPLE MEANS OF REPRESENTATION:

There is no right answer as to which strategy is the best or most efficient for a given problem type. Different students may find certain strategies easier than others. Allow for creativity in modeling, expressing, and critiquing different solution strategies; however, acknowledge that some students may feel most comfortable and capable using a particular method.

Take the students through the process of solving the problem by relating the chip model to the algorithm, renaming 605 as 5 hundreds, 9 tens, 15 ones in one step. When finished, engage students in a discussion about which methods they prefer.

Instruct the students to work in pairs through the following problems, discussing which strategy they think would work best for each problem: 500 − 257, 702 − 195, 600 − 314. As students demonstrate proficiency renaming in one step, instruct them to work on the Problem Set.

Problem Set (10 minutes)

Students should do their personal best to complete the Problem Set within the allotted 10 minutes. For some classes, it may be appropriate to modify the assignment by specifying which problems they work on first. Some problems do not specify a method for solving. Students solve these problems using the RDW approach used for Application Problems.

Student Debrief (10 minutes)

Lesson Objective: Apply and explain alternate methods for subtracting from multiples of 100 and from numbers with zero in the tens place.

The Student Debrief is intended to invite reflection and active processing of the total lesson experience.

Invite students to review their solutions for the Problem Set. They should check work by comparing answers with a partner before going over answers as a class. Look for

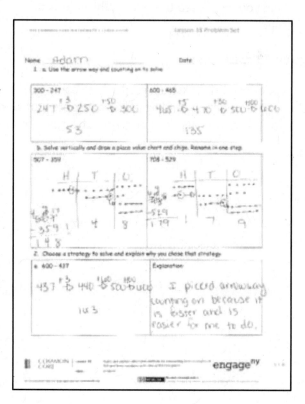

COMMON CORE™   **Lesson 18:**   Apply and explain alternate methods for subtracting from multiples of 100 and from numbers with zero in the tens place.   **5.C.70**

                                  Date: 10/23/13

MP.3

misconceptions or misunderstandings that can be addressed in the Debrief. Guide students in a conversation to debrief the Problem Set and process the lesson.

You may choose to use any combination of the questions below to lead the discussion.

- For Problem 1(a), how did you use the arrow way to solve? What did you add on first to efficiently solve each problem? Why?

- For Problem 1(b), explain the meaning of the 9 in the tens place. Where is the other ten?

- For Problem 2(a), 600 – 437, explain the strategy you chose to solve? Why was using the arrow way easier than subtracting using the algorithm?

- For Problem 2(b), 808 – 597, how did you rename 808 for subtraction? What does that look like using the algorithm? Or, why did you choose to solve mentally?

- For Problem 3(a), how does the smiling student use compensation to make the subtraction problem much simpler? Why is this strategy a good choice here?

- How did you use compensation to solve Problems 3(b) and (c)? What other simplifying strategies could you have used to solve? Which do you prefer?

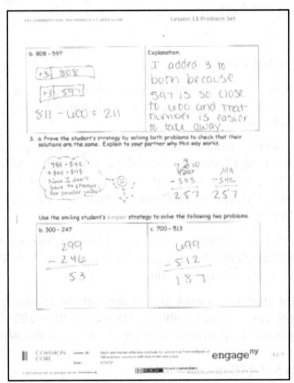

Exit Ticket (3 minutes)

After the Student Debrief, instruct students to complete the Exit Ticket. A review of their work will help you assess the students' understanding of the concepts that were presented in the lesson today and plan more effectively for future lessons. You may read the questions aloud to the students.

COMMON CORE   **Lesson 18:**   Apply and explain alternate methods for subtracting from multiples of 100 and from numbers with zero in the tens place.

Date: 10/23/13

5.C.71

Name _____ Date _____

1.

    a. Use the arrow way and counting on to solve.

300 – 247	600 – 465

    b. Solve vertically and draw a place value chart and chips. Rename in one step.

507 – 359	708 – 529

2. Choose a strategy to solve and explain why you chose that strategy.

a. 600 – 437	Explanation:

Lesson 18:   Apply and explain alternate methods for subtracting from multiples of 100 and from numbers with zero in the tens place.

Date: 10/23/13

b. 808 – 597	Explanation:

3.

a. Prove the student's strategy by solving both problems to check that their solutions are the same. Explain to your partner why this way works.

Use the smiling student's simpler strategy to solve the following two problems.

b. 300 – 247	c. 700 – 513

COMMON CORE™   Lesson 18:   Apply and explain alternate methods for subtracting from multiples of 100 and from numbers with zero in the tens place.

Date: 10/23/13

5.C.73

Name _____   Date _____

Choose a strategy to solve and explain why you chose that strategy.

1. 400 – 265	Explanation:
2. 507 – 198	Explanation:

COMMON CORE™ | **Lesson 18:** | Apply and explain alternate methods for subtracting from multiples of 100 and from numbers with zero in the tens place. | 5.C.74
| **Date:** | 10/23/13 |

© 2013 Common Core, Inc. All rights reserved. commoncore.org

Name _____   Date _____

1.

a. Use the arrow way and counting on to solve.

700 - 462	900 - 232

b. Solve vertically and draw a place value chart and chips. Rename in one step.

907 - 467	803 - 667

2. Choose a strategy to solve and explain why you chose that strategy.

a. 700 – 390	Explanation:

COMMON CORE™

Lesson 18:   Apply and explain alternate methods for subtracting from multiples of
100 and from numbers with zero in the tens place.
Date: 10/23/13

5.C.75

b. 919 – 657

Explanation:

3.

a. Explain why 300 – 186 is the same as 299 – 185.

b. Solve 500 – 278 using the simplifying strategy from (a).

Lesson 18:

Date:

Apply and explain alternate methods for subtracting from multiples of
100 and from numbers with zero in the tens place.

10/23/13

5.C.76

Topic D

Student Explanations for Choice of Solution Methods

2.NBT.7, 2.NBT.8, 2.NBT.9

Focus Standards:	2.NBT.7	Add and subtract within 1000, using concrete models or drawings and strategies based on place value, properties of operations, and/or the relationship between addition and subtraction; relate the strategy to a written method. Understand that in adding or subtracting three-digit numbers, one adds or subtracts hundreds and hundreds, tens and tens, ones and ones; and sometimes it is necessary to compose or decompose tens or hundreds.
	2.NBT.8	Mentally add 10 or 100 to a given number 100–900, and mentally subtract 10 or 100 from a given number 100–900.
	2.NBT.9	Explain why addition and subtraction strategies work, using place value and the properties of operations. (Explanations may be supported by drawings or objects.)
Instructional Days:	2	
Coherence -Links from:	G1–M2	Introduction to Place Value Through Addition and Subtraction Within 20
-Links to:	G3–M2	Place Value and Problem Solving with Units of Measure

Topic D focuses on the application of the tools and concepts presented in Topics A through C. Students synthesize their understanding of addition and subtraction strategies, and then use that understanding to determine which of those strategies to apply to a variety of problems, including number bond problems and problems with the unknown in all positions (e.g., 200 + _____ = 342, _____ − 53 = 400).

Students then discuss and analyze their chosen methods and decide which method is most efficient for the given problem type. For example, when digits are close to the next ten or hundred (e.g., 530 − _____ = 390), some students might use related addition and mentally add on tens and hundreds, while others might solve the same problem using arrow notation.

Working with these problems provides a sound foundation for future work with word problems. Listening to peer explanations can make certain strategies more accessible for struggling students, and allows more time and practice to achieve mastery.

A Teaching Sequence Towards Mastery of Student Explanations for Choice of Solution Methods
Objective 1: **Choose and explain solution strategies and record with a written addition or subtraction method.** **(Lessons 19–20)**

Lesson 19

Objective: Choose and explain solution strategies and record with a written addition or subtraction method.

Suggested Lesson Structure

■ Fluency Practice   (12 minutes)
▢ Concept Development   (38 minutes)
■ Student Debrief   (10 minutes)
  Total Time   **(60 minutes)**

Fluency Practice (12 minutes)

- Grade 2 Core Fluency Differentiated Practice **2.OA.2**   (5 minutes)
- Take from the Ten **2.OA.2**   (3 minutes)
- Skip Counting by Twos **2.OA.3**   (4 minutes)

Grade 2 Core Fluency Differentiated Practice Sets (5 minutes)

Materials: (S) Core Fluency Practice Sets

Note: During Topic C and for the remainder of the year, each day's fluency includes an opportunity for review and mastery of the sums and differences with totals through 20 by means of the Core Fluency Practice Sets or Sprints.

Take from the Ten (3 minutes)

Materials: Personal white boards

Note: Students practice taking from the ten in order to subtract fluently within 20.

   T: I say, "11 – 9." You write, "10 – 9 + 1." Wait for my signal. Ready?
   T: 12 – 8. Show me your boards on my signal.
   S: 10 – 8 + 2.
   T: Write your answer.
   S: 4.

Continue with the following possible sequence: 13 – 9, 14 – 8, 12 – 9, 11 – 8, 15 – 9, 11 – 7, 16 – 8, 17 – 9, 13 – 7.

Lesson 19:   Choose and explain solution strategies and record with a written
               addition or subtraction method.
Date: 10/23/13

5.D.3

Skip-Counting by Twos (4 minutes)

Note: Students practice counting by twos in anticipation of learning the foundations of multiplication and division in Module 6.

T: Let's skip-count by twos. On my signal, count by ones from 0 to 20 in a whisper. Ready? (Tap the desk while the students are counting, knock on the twos. For example, tap, knock, tap, knock, etc.)

T: Did anyone notice what I was doing while you were counting? I was tapping by ones but I knocked on every other number. Let's count again and try knocking and tapping with me.

S: 1 (tap), 2 (knock), 3 (tap), 4 (knock), 5 (tap), 6 (knock), etc.

Continue this routine up to 20.

Concept Development (38 minutes)

Materials: (S) Personal white boards, number disks (if appropriate for student level)

This lesson gives students the opportunity to choose which strategies to apply to a variety of addition and subtraction problems, and to explain their choices and listen to the reasoning of their peers. In order to allow for this in-depth conversation, the Application Problem has been omitted from G2–M5–Lessons 19–20.

The conversation can be structured as a whole group, in teams of four, or in partners, depending on what is best for a given class.

Problem 1: 180 + 440

Give students three minutes to solve the problem using the strategy of their choice. Then, invite students to share their work and reasoning.

T: Turn and talk: Explain your strategy and why you chose it to your small group.

S1: I used a chip model to represent the hundreds and tens for each number, because there were no ones. Then I added the tens together and the hundreds together. Since there were 12 tens, I renamed it as a hundred, with 2 tens leftover. So, my answer was 620.

S2: I used the arrow way. I started with 180, added on 400 to get 580, then added on 20 to make 600, and 20 more is 620.

S3: I used a number bond to take apart 440. I took 20 from the 440 and added it to 180 to make 200. 200 plus 420 is 620.

T: Turn and talk. How efficient were the strategies we used and why?

$$180 \xrightarrow{+400} 580 \xrightarrow{+20} 600 \xrightarrow{+20} 620$$

Lesson 19:   Choose and explain solution strategies and record with a written addition or subtraction method.

Date: 10/23/13

5.D.4

© 2013 Common Core, Inc. All rights reserved. commoncore.org

S: I think the arrow way was efficient because he did it in his head.
→ I think the number bond was good because adding onto 500
is easy. → I think the chip model is inefficient because it took a
long time to draw all the chips and with easy numbers you can
do it faster in your head.

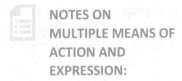

Consider facilitating a discussion about recognizing a problem that is
efficiently solved without the algorithm or math drawings. For example, students should recognize that
when adding two numbers with only hundreds and tens, mental math or a simplifying strategy is the best
option.

Problem 2: 400 – 236

Give students three minutes to solve the problem using the strategy of their choice.

T: Explain your strategy and why you chose it to your small group. Turn and talk.

S1: I used a tape diagram to subtract one from each number so I can subtract without renaming.
399 – 235 is 164.

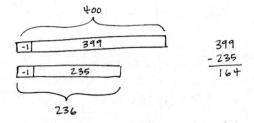

S2: I used the arrow way to count up from 236 to 400. I
started at 236 and added 4 to make 240, then I added
60 more to get to 300. Then I added 1 hundred to
make 400. I added 164 altogether.

$$236 \xrightarrow{+4} 240 \xrightarrow{+60} 300 \xrightarrow{+100} 400$$

$$4 + 60 + 100 = 164$$

S3: I just used the algorithm, because I already know that when I have zeros in the tens and ones places, I
can rename the whole easily. I changed 400 to 3 hundreds, 9 tens, and 10 ones. Then, I subtracted. I
also got 164.

T: Turn and talk. How was drawing the chip model
similar to solving with the algorithm?

S: They are the same except that Student 1 also
used a math drawing to decompose 500. →
Student 1's work shows Student 3's work in a
picture. → You can see that 500 was broken
apart into 4 hundreds, 9 tens, 10 ones to set up for subtraction.

  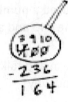

**NOTES ON
MULTIPLE MEANS OF
ACTION AND
EXPRESSION:**

Encourage For students who answer
mental math over and over to the
question of which strategy is most
efficient to describe which simplifying
strategy they used mentally. Explain
that they need to show their work on
assessments, so they will need to
practice writing it down.

	Lesson 19:	Choose and explain solution strategies and record with a written	5.D.5
		addition or subtraction method.	
	Date:	10/23/13	

T: Turn and talk. How efficient were the strategies we used and why?

S: I think the arrow way was super-efficient because it was just hop to 240, hop to 300, and hop to 400.
→ The chip model was slow but safe, too, because he was able to check his work easily with the
drawing. → I think the algorithm was less efficient for me because without the drawing I ended up
getting the answer wrong and I had to redo it.

Problem 3: 389 + 411

T: (Allow students three minutes to work the problem.) Explain your strategy and why you chose it to
your small group. Turn and Talk.

S1: I used a chip model because I saw that I am adding two three-digit numbers. I drew and then added
the ones to make a ten, then I added the tens to make a hundred, then I added the hundreds. I
recorded my work using new groups below. My answer is 800.

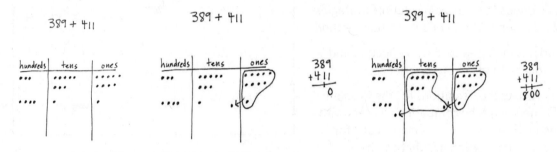

S2: I chose to use the arrow way because I saw that 389 has 9 in the ones place and 411 has 1 in the
ones place, so I knew I would be making a ten. I started at 389 and added 1 to get 390, then I added
10 to get 400, then I added 400 and I got 800. It fit like a puzzle.

$$389 \xrightarrow{+1} 390 \xrightarrow{+10} 400 \xrightarrow{+400} 800$$

S3: I decided to use a number bond because I noticed that 389 needs 11 to
get to 400 and that 411 has 11! So then I knew a number bond was best.
I took 11 from 411 and added it to 389 to get 400, then I added 400 to get
800.

T: Turn and talk. How efficient were the strategies we used and why?

S: I think the chip model was slow but good for me because then I didn't
lose track of making 10 and making 100. → I think the arrow way was great because it is easy to add
on the 411 after you take it apart. → I think the number bond was efficient because 11 and 389
makes 400 really easily. Then you just add on 400 more and you're done!

If students are ready to move on to the Problem Set, allow them to begin. If they need more discussion,
continue the above sequence with the following problems: 275 + 125, 672 − 458, 377 + 350.

	Lesson 19:	Choose and explain solution strategies and record with a written addition or subtraction method.	5.D.6
	Date:	10/23/13	

Problem Set (10 minutes)

Students should do their personal best to complete the Problem Set within the allotted 10 minutes. For some classes, it may be appropriate to modify the assignment by specifying which problems they work on first. Some problems do not specify a method for solving. Students solve these problems using the RDW approach used for Application Problems.

Student Debrief (10 minutes)

Lesson Objective: Choose and explain solution strategies and record with a written addition or subtraction method.

The Student Debrief is intended to invite reflection and active processing of the total lesson experience.

Invite students to review their solutions for the Problem Set. They should check work by comparing answers with a partner before going over answers as a class. Look for misconceptions or misunderstandings that can be addressed in the Debrief. Guide students in a conversation to debrief the Problem Set and process the lesson.

You may choose to use any combination of the questions below to lead the discussion.

- Share with a partner: For Problems 1(a) and (b), explain and compare the two strategies used to solve 500 – 211.

- For Problem 1, how could you arrive at the same answer using a different solution strategy? Share and compare with a partner.

- For Problem 2(a), how did you solve? Why? In your opinion, which one is most efficient?

- For Problem 2(b), did you use an addition or subtraction method to solve? Explain your thinking. Can you think of an alternate strategy?

- For Problem 2(c), what were you thinking when you selected a solution strategy to solve? How does knowing your partners to 10 help you to solve quickly?

- For Problem 2(d), what is challenging about solving this problem using the algorithm? How could you change this into a simpler problem?

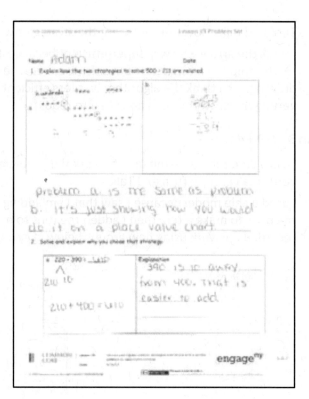

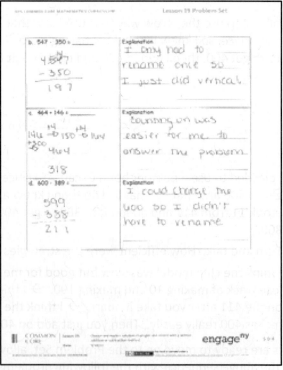

COMMON CORE

Lesson 19: Choose and explain solution strategies and record with a written addition or subtraction method.

Date: 10/23/13

5.D.7

Exit Ticket (3 minutes)

After the Student Debrief, instruct students to complete the Exit Ticket. A review of their work will help you assess the students' understanding of the concepts that were presented in the lesson today and plan more effectively for future lessons. You may read the questions aloud to the students.

Lesson 19:   Choose and explain solution strategies and record with a written
              addition or subtraction method.

Date: 10/23/13

5.D.8

Name _____ Date _____

1. Explain how the two strategies to solve 500 − 211 are related.

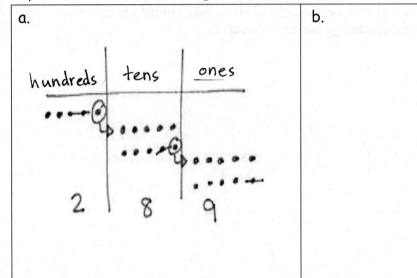

a.

b.

_____

_____

_____

2. Solve and explain why you chose that strategy.

a. 220 + 390 = _____

Explanation:

_____

_____

_____

_____

Lesson 19: Choose and explain solution strategies and record with a written
addition or subtraction method.

Date: 10/23/13.

5.D.9

b. 547 – 350 = _____

Explanation:

_____

_____

_____

_____

c. 464 + 146 = _____

Explanation:

_____

_____

_____

_____

d. 600 – 389 = _____

Explanation:

_____

_____

_____

_____

COMMON CORE™

Lesson 19: Choose and explain solution strategies and record with a written
addition or subtraction method.

Date: 10/23/13

5.D.10

Name _____ Date _____

Solve and explain why you chose that strategy.

1. 400 + 590 = _____	Explanation: _____ _____ _____ _____
2. 775 – 497 = _____	Explanation: _____ _____ _____ _____

COMMON CORE™

Lesson 19: Choose and explain solution strategies and record with a written addition or subtraction method.
Date: 10/23/13

5.D.11

Name _____   Date _____

1. Solve and explain why you chose that strategy.

340 + 250 = _____	Explanation: _____ _____ _____ _____
490 + 350 = _____	Explanation: _____ _____ _____ _____
519 + 342	Explanation: _____ _____ _____ _____

  Lesson 19:   Choose and explain solution strategies and record with a written
                                  addition or subtraction method.
          Date: 10/23/13

5.D.12

610 + _____ = 784	Explanation:
700 – 456 = _____	Explanation:
904 – 395 = _____	Explanation:

COMMON CORE™

Lesson 19: Choose and explain solution strategies and record with a written addition or subtraction method.
Date: 10/23/13

5.D.13

Lesson 20

Objective: Choose and explain solution strategies and record with a written addition or subtraction method.

Suggested Lesson Structure

■ Fluency Practice   (12 minutes)

☐ Concept Development   (38 minutes)

■ Student Debrief   (10 minutes)

  Total Time   **(60 minutes)**

Fluency Practice (12 minutes)

- Grade 2 Core Fluency Differentiated Practice **2.OA.2**   (5 minutes)
- Take from the Ten **2.OA.2**   (3 minutes)
- Skip Counting by Twos **2.OA.3**   (4 minutes)

Grade 2 Core Fluency Differentiated Practice Sets (5 minutes)

Materials: (S) Core Fluency Practice Sets

Note: During Topic C and for the remainder of the year, each day's fluency includes an opportunity for review and mastery of the sums and differences with totals through 20 by means of the Core Fluency Practice Sets or Sprints.

Take from the Ten (3 minutes)

Materials: Personal white boards

Note: Students practice taking from the ten in order to subtract fluently within 20.

   T: I say, "11 – 9." You write, "10 – 9 + 1." Wait for my signal. Ready?

   T: 12 – 8. Show me your boards on my signal.

   S: 10 – 8 + 2.

   T: Write your answer.

   S: 4.

Continue with the following possible sequence: 13 – 9, 14 – 8, 12 – 9, 11 – 8, 15 – 9, 11 – 7, 16 – 8, 17 – 9, 13 – 7.

Lesson 20:   Choose and explain solution strategies and record with a written
                  addition or subtraction method.
Date: 10/23/13

5.D.14

Skip-Counting by Twos (4 minutes)

Note: Students practice counting by twos in anticipation of learning the foundations of multiplication and division in module 6.

> T: Let's skip-count by twos. On my signal, count by ones from 0 to 20 in a whisper. Ready? (Tap the desk while the students are counting, knock on the twos. For example, tap, knock, tap, knock, etc.)
>
> T: Did anyone notice what I was doing while you were counting? I was tapping by ones but I knocked on every other number. Let's count again and try knocking and tapping with me.
>
> S: 1 (tap), 2 (knock), 3 (tap), 4 (knock), 5 (tap), 6 (knock), etc.

Continue this routine up to 20.

Concept Development (38 minutes)

Materials: (S) Personal white boards, number disks (if appropriate for student levels)

This lesson again gives students the opportunity to talk about their understanding of addition and subtraction strategies and to choose which strategies to apply to a variety of problems. In order to allow for this talk, the Application Problem has been omitted from G2–M5–Lessons 19–20.

Problem 1: 499 + 166

Invite students to solve the problem using a strategy of their choice as they did in G2–M5–Lesson 19. Give them three minutes to solve the problem. Then, instruct them to find a partner who used a different strategy to solve. Invite one set of partners up to the board and lead them through the following conversation:

> T: Partner 1, teach your strategy to your partner and explain why you chose that strategy.
>
> S1: I used a number bond since 499 is so close to 500. I took 1 from 166 and added it to 499 to get 500; then I added on the rest to get 665.
>
> T: Partner 2, teach your strategy to your partner and explain why you chose that strategy.
>
> S2: I used the arrow way, because it's easy to add on from 499. I added on a hundred, then 1 more to make 600, then 65 more. So, I also got 665.
>
> T: (Point to student drawings on the board.) How were the strategies they used similar and how were they different? Turn and talk with your partner.
>
> S: They both decomposed 166. → Partner 1 tried to make friendly numbers, like 500. And Partner 2 broke apart 166 and added on parts. → Both partners used a simplifying strategy. → Both partners added 1 to make the next hundred. But Partner 1 made 500, and Partner 2 made 600.
>
> T: Did both strategies work?
>
> S: Yes!

$$499 + 166$$
$$\diagup\ \diagdown$$
$$1\quad 165$$

$$500 + 165 = 665$$

$$499 \xrightarrow{+100} 599 \xrightarrow{+1} 600 \xrightarrow{65} 665$$

Instruct partners to engage in a conversation similar to the one modeled above. After partners finish sharing strategies and rationale, give each student a few minutes to solve the problem using her partner's strategy. Circulate and provide support, while students check each other's work before returning to their seats for the next problem.

NOTES ON
MULTIPLE MEANS OF
ACTION
AND EXPRESSION:

For more introverted students or those who find spoken communication in groups challenging, allow them to write their explanations or to discuss their solutions with a trusted friend.

T: I noticed that very few of you solved using chips or the algorithm. Would that strategy also be efficient?

S: Well, you would have to rename twice. → You should always try to solve mentally if you are close to a hundred. → I can picture the number bond in my head now, and it's easy to add on once you make 500.

T: I hear some thoughtful responses! Let's take a look at another problem.

Problem 2: 546 – 297

Give students three minutes to solve using a strategy of their choice. Then, instruct them to find a partner who used a different solution strategy. Prompt them to engage in a conversation similar to the one modeled above.

T: Class, after you solve and find a partner who used a *different* strategy, I'd like you to share and explain your strategies.

(Circulate and listen.)

S1: I used compensation and added 3 to both numbers, so that I could subtract 300 instead of 297. So, 549 minus 300 equals 249. Easy!

S2: I used the algorithm to solve, because I know the steps, so it doesn't take me long. After drawing my magnifying glass, I decomposed twice, because there weren't enough tens or ones to subtract. I renamed 546 as 4 hundreds, 13 tens, 16 ones. Then I subtracted hundreds, tens, and ones, and I got 249.

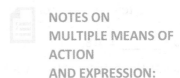

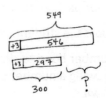

$$549 - 300 = 249$$

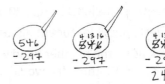

T: Turn and talk to your partner: How efficient were the strategies you used and why?

S: I like the algorithm, because it has steps, and it works every time. → Making friendly numbers is a good strategy, because you can very easily take away 300 from 549 in your head.

NOTES ON
MULTIPLE MEANS OF
REPRESENTATION:

Post a list of these strategies and examples on the board so students who are still learning the strategies can refer to it.

T: How were the strategies you discussed similar and how were they different? Turn and talk to your partner.

S: We both used subtraction to solve. → I used a drawing, and my partner just used the algorithm. → I used renaming, but my partner used compensation to make a hundred.

After partners finish sharing strategies and rationale, each student takes a few minutes to solve the problem

Lesson 20:   Choose and explain solution strategies and record with a written
             addition or subtraction method.
Date: 10/23/13

5.D.16

using his partner's strategy. While the teacher circulates and provides support, students check each other's work before returning to their seats for the next problem.

Problem 3: 320 + _____ = 418

Again, give students three minutes to solve before finding a partner who used a different solution strategy. Prompt partners to engage in a conversation by following these steps:

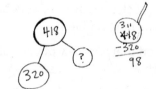

1. Share and explain your strategy to your partner.
2. Listen to your partner's strategy.
3. Practice solving using your partner's strategy.
4. Decide if your strategies are efficient.
5. Discuss how your strategies are similar and how they are different.
6. Compliment your partner about his work. Be specific!

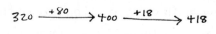

The following reflects possible student explanations:

- I drew a number bond to show the missing part, and then I used related subtraction to solve. I thought drawing a number bond was a good idea, because it helped me know where to start to find the answer.

- I used the arrow way to count on to 418. I knew by looking at the problem that I had to add on to 320 to get to 418. I started by adding 80 to get to 400. Then I added a ten and 8 ones. Altogether I added 98. So, 320 plus 98 equals 418.

The following reflects possible student discussion:

- I think using the number bond was a good idea, because it helps me to see the parts and the whole. → Another idea would be to draw the number bond and then count on to solve. → If you used the arrow way you could add on 100 and then just take back 2.

- I solved using addition, but you solved with subtraction. → We both knew that 320 was one part, and we were trying to find the missing part. → I counted up to get to 418, and you started with 418 and subtracted one part.

The sample responses demonstrate students developing flexibility in their application of strategies to solve varied problems. Encourage students to consider the strategies they used and how they could adapt them to best meet their own needs.

If students need more practice, continue with one or more problems from the following suggested sequence: 334 + 143, 538 + 180, 450 + _____ = 688, 746 − _____ = 510. Otherwise, allow them to begin the Problem Set.

Problem Set (10 minutes)

Students should do their personal best to complete the Problem Set within the allotted 10 minutes. For some classes, it may be appropriate to modify the assignment by specifying which problems they work on first. Some problems do not specify a method for solving. Students solve these problems using the RDW approach used for Application Problems.

Lesson 20:   Choose and explain solution strategies and record with a written
             addition or subtraction method.
Date: 10/23/13

5.D.17

Student Debrief (10 minutes)

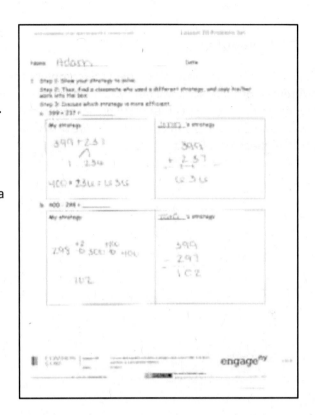

Lesson Objective: Choose and explain solution strategies and record with a written addition or subtraction method.

The Student Debrief is intended to invite reflection and active processing of the total lesson experience.

Invite students to review their solutions for the Problem Set. They should check work by comparing answers with a partner before going over answers as a class. Look for misconceptions or misunderstandings that can be addressed in the Debrief. Guide students in a conversation to debrief the Problem Set and process the lesson.

You may choose to use any combination of the questions below to lead the discussion.

- For Problem 1(a), which mental or simplifying strategy did you choose to solve? Why? How was this different from your partner's strategy?

- For Problem 1(b), did you choose a mental strategy or the algorithm to solve? Why?

- Look at Problem 1(c). Compare your strategy to your partner's. Which one was more efficient? Defend your reasoning.

- Turn and talk. For Problem 1(d), did you solve using addition or subtraction? Why? Explain your reasoning using pictures, number, and words.

- What are all the possible ways to solve Problem 1(e)? Which one do you prefer?

- Which solution strategies are fastest and easiest for you? Why?

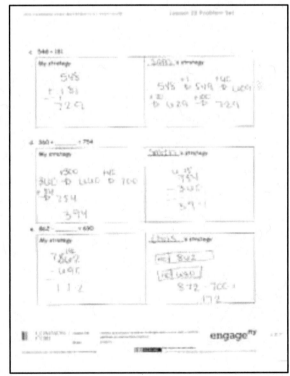

COMMON CORE

Lesson 20: Choose and explain solution strategies and record with a written addition or subtraction method.
Date: 10/23/13

5.D.18

Exit Ticket (3 minutes)

After the Student Debrief, instruct students to complete the Exit Ticket. A review of their work will help you assess the students' understanding of the concepts that were presented in the lesson today and plan more effectively for future lessons. You may read the questions aloud to the students.

NOTES ON MULTIPLE MEANS OF ACTION AND EXPRESSION:

For more introverted students or those who find spoken communication in groups challenging, allow them to write their explanations or to discuss their solutions with a trusted friend.

COMMON CORE™

Lesson 20: Choose and explain solution strategies and record with a written addition or subtraction method.

Date: 10/23/13

5.D.19

Name _____   Date _____

1. Step 1:   Show your strategy to solve.

    Step 2:   Find a classmate who used a different strategy, and copy his work into the box.

    Step 3:   Discuss which strategy is more efficient.

a. 399 + 237 = _____

My strategy	_____'s strategy

b. 400 - 298 = _____

My strategy	_____'s strategy

c. 548 + 181

My strategy	_____'s strategy

d. 360 + _____ = 754

My strategy	_____'s strategy

e. 862 - _____ = 690

My strategy	_____'s strategy

COMMON CORE   **Lesson 20:**   Choose and explain solution strategies and record with a written addition or subtraction method.

Date: 10/23/13

5.D.21

Name _____   Date _____

Solve each problem using two different strategies.

1. 299 + 156 = _____

First Strategy	Second Strategy

2. 547 + _____ = 841

First Strategy	Second Strategy

COMMON CORE™   **Lesson 20:**   Choose and explain solution strategies and record with a written
addition or subtraction method.   5.D.22

Date: 10/23/13

Name _____ Date _____

1. Solve each problem using two different strategies.

   a. 456 + 244 = _____

First Strategy	Second Strategy

   b. 698 + _____ = 945

First Strategy	Second Strategy

COMMON CORE™ | Lesson 20:   Choose and explain solution strategies and record with a written
addition or subtraction method.   5.D.23
                     | Date: 10/23/13

2. Circle a strategy to solve and explain why you chose that strategy.

    a. 257 + 160

Arrow way / Algorithm

Solve.	Explanation:
	_____
	_____
	_____
	_____
	_____

    b. 754 - 597

Number bond / Arrow way

Solve.	Explanation:
	_____
	_____
	_____
	_____
	_____

COMMON CORE   Lesson 20:   Choose and explain solution strategies and record with a written addition or subtraction method.   **5.D.24**

Date: 10/23/13

Name _____   Date _____

1. Solve each problem with a written strategy such as a tape diagram, a number bond, the arrow way, the vertical method, or chips on a place value chart.

a. 220 + 30 = _____	b. 200 + 380 = _____	c. 450 + 210 = _____
d. 490 + 12 = _____	e. _____ = 380 + 220	f. 750 – 590 = _____

2. Use the arrow way to solve.

a.	b.	c.
$342 \xrightarrow{+100} \text{_____} \xrightarrow{+\text{\_\_\_}} 542$	$600 \xrightarrow{-\text{\_\_\_}} 500 \xrightarrow{-\text{\_\_\_}} 490$	$\text{\_\_\_\_} \xrightarrow{+100} \text{\_\_\_\_} \xrightarrow{+10} 768$
d. 542 + 207 = _____	e. 430 + 361 = _____	f. 660 – 190 = _____

3. Solve each by drawing a model of a place value chart with chips and the vertical method.

a. 328 + 259 = _____	b. 575 + 345 = _____

Circle **True or False** for each number sentence. Explain your thinking using pictures, words, or numbers.

c. 466 + 244 = 600 + 100 **True / False**	d. 690 + 179 = 700 + 169 **True / False**

e.	f.
398 + 6 = 400 + 5	724 − 298 = 722 + 300
True / False	**True / False**

4. Solve each problem with two written strategies such as a tape diagram, a number bond, the arrow way, the vertical method, or chips on a place value chart.

a. 299 + 436 = _____	
b. 470 + 390 = _____	

c. 268 + 122 = _____

d. 330 – 190 = _____

      Topics A–B

Use Place Value Understanding and Properties of Operations to Add and Subtract

2.NBT.7   Add and subtract within 1000, using concrete models or drawings and strategies based on place value, properties of operations, and/or the relationship between addition and subtraction; relates the strategy to a written method. Understand that in adding and subtracting three-digit numbers, one adds or subtracts hundreds and hundreds, tens and tens, ones and ones; and sometimes it is necessary to compose or decompose tens or hundreds.

2.NBT.8   Mentally add 10 or 100 to a given number 100–900, and mentally subtract 10 or 100 from a given number 100–900.

2.NBT.9   Explain why addition and subtraction strategies work, using place value and the properties of operations. (Explanations may be supported by drawings or objects.)

Evaluating Student Learning Outcomes

A Progression Toward Mastery is provided to describe steps that illuminate the gradually increasing understandings that students develop *on their way to proficiency.* In this chart, this progress is presented from left (Step 1) to right (Step 4). The learning goal for each student is to achieve Step 4 mastery. These steps are meant to help teachers and students identify and celebrate what the student CAN do now and what they need to work on next.

A Progression Toward Mastery

Assessment Task Item and Standards Assessed	STEP 1 Little evidence of reasoning without a correct answer. (1 Point)	STEP 2 Evidence of some reasoning without a correct answer. (2 Points)	STEP 3 Evidence of some reasoning with a correct answer or evidence of solid reasoning with an incorrect answer. (3 Points)	STEP 4 Evidence of solid reasoning with a correct answer. (4 Points)
1 2.NBT.7 2.NBT.8	The student provides one to two correct answers with correct strategies *or* provides up to six correct answers with no concrete representation.	The student answers three to four parts correctly by using a suggested strategy.	The student solves five out of six parts correctly by using a suggested strategy.	The student correctly shows a strategy to solve: a. 250 b. 580 c. 660 d. 502 e. 600 f. 160
2 2.NBT.7 2.NBT.8	The student solves one to two out of six parts correctly by using the arrow way, *or* solves all six parts correctly but does not use the arrow way.	The student solves three to four out of six parts correctly by using the arrow way, *or* provides a correct answer on up to six parts but only uses the arrow way for three parts.	The student solves five out of six parts correctly by using the arrow way.	The student correctly models the arrow way and solves to find: a. 442, +100 b. -100, -10 c. 658, 758 d. 749 e. 791 f. 470

3
 	
2.NBT.7
2.NBT.9
	The student solves one or two out of six parts correctly with or without a chip model and with or without providing a written explanation.	The student attempts to use a chip model to answer Parts (a) and (b) but arrives at an incorrect answer, *and* the student shows no explanation for Parts (c), (d), (e), and (f) but correctly answers true or false, *or* the student provides some explanation for Parts (c), (d), (e), and (f) but their explanation is incorrect.	The student solves five out of six parts correctly by using a chip model for Parts (a) and (b) or explaining using pictures, numbers, or words for Parts (c), (d), (e), (f).	The student correctly:
				
				▪ Models with place value chips and the vertical method to solve:
				
				  a. 587
				  b. 920
				
				▪ Explains using pictures, numbers, or words to solve:
				
				  c. False
				  d. True
				  e. False

A Progression Toward Mastery

				f. False
4 **2.NBT.7** **2.NBT.8** **2.NBT.9**	The student solves one problem correctly with or without a written strategy.	The student solves two problems correctly by using a strategy correctly, *or* the student solves two or more problems correctly without any strategy shown.	The student solves all four problems correctly and shows six to seven correct strategies, or the student solves three out of the four problems correctly with six correct strategies.	The student correctly uses two different strategies to solve: a. 735 b. 860 c. 390 d. 140

Name   *Andy*   Date   *Jan. 4*

1. Solve each problem with a written strategy such as: a tape diagram, number bond, the arrow way, the vertical method, or chips on a place value chart.

a. 220 + 30 = **250** $$220 \xrightarrow{+30} 250$$	b. 200 + 380 = **580** $$380 \xrightarrow{+200} 580$$	c. 450 + 210 = **660** $$450 \xrightarrow{+200} 650 \xrightarrow{+10} 660$$
d. 490 + 12 = **502** $$\overset{10 \quad 2}{\frown}$$ $$500 + 2 = 502$$	e. **600** = 380 + 220 $$\overset{20 \quad 200}{\frown}$$ $$400 + 200$$	f. 750 - 590 = **160** 760 $$\begin{array}{c} \boxed{\begin{array}{c} 750 \\ \hline 590 \end{array}} \end{array}$$ +10 ... +10 600 $$760 - 600 = 160$$

2. Use the arrow way to solve.

a. $$342 \xrightarrow{+100} 442 \xrightarrow{+100} 542$$	b. $$600 \xrightarrow{-100} 500 \xrightarrow{-10} 490$$	c. $$658 \xrightarrow{+100} 758 \xrightarrow{+10} 768$$
d. 542 + 207 = **749** $$542 \xrightarrow{+200} 742 \xrightarrow{+7} 749$$	e. 430 + 361 = **791** $$361 \xrightarrow{+400} 761 \xrightarrow{+30} 791$$	f. 660 - 190 = **470** $$660 \xrightarrow{-200} 460 \xrightarrow{+10} 470$$

3. Solve each by drawing a model of a place value chart and chips and the vertical method.

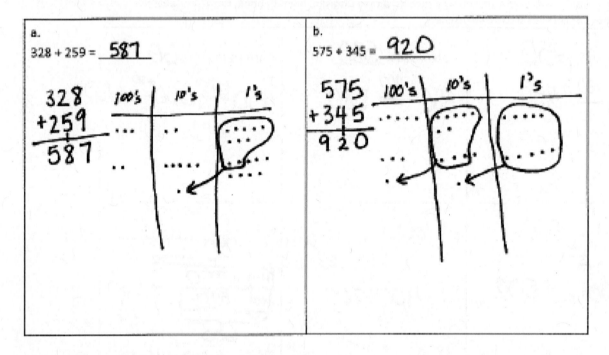

a.

328 + 259 = __587__

b.

575 + 345 = __920__

Circle **True** or **False** for each number sentence. Explain your thinking using pictures, words or numbers.

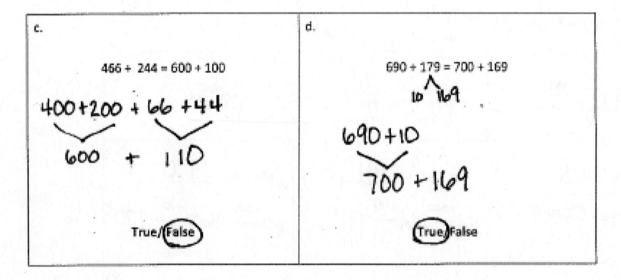

c.

466 + 244 = 600 + 100

True/**False**

d.

690 + 179 = 700 + 169

True/False

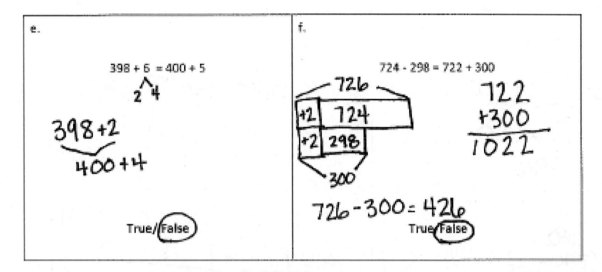

e.

398 + 6 = 400 + 5

$2\overset{\wedge}{}4$

398+2

400+4

True/**False**

f.

724 - 298 = 722 + 300

726
+2 724
+2 298
300

722
+300
1022

726 - 300 = 426

True/**False**

4. Solve each problem with two written strategies such as: a tape diagram, number bond, the arrow way, the vertical method, or chips on a place value chart.

a. 299 + 436 = **735**

436 $\xrightarrow{+300}$ 736 $\xrightarrow{-1}$ 735

299 + 436

$1\overset{\wedge}{}435$

299 + 1 + 435

300 + 435

735

b. 470 + 390 = **860**

470 + 390

460 $\overset{\wedge}{}$ 10

460 + 400

860

390 $\xrightarrow{+10}$ 400 $\xrightarrow{+60}$ 460 $\xrightarrow{+400}$ 860

c. 268 + 122 = **390**

| 268 | 2 | 120 |

270 + 120
390

268 $\xrightarrow{+2}$ 270 $\xrightarrow{+20}$ 290 $\xrightarrow{+100}$ 390

d. 330 - 190 = **140**

340
+10 330
+10 190
200

340 - 200 = 140

100's	10's	1's
- X O	. . .	
1	4	0

Name _____　　Date _____

1. Solve each problem with a written strategy such as a tape diagram, a number bond, the arrow way, the vertical method, or chips on a place value chart.

a. 460 + 200 = _____	b. _____ = 865 − 300	c. _____ + 400 = 598
d. 240 − 190 = _____	e. _____ = 760 − 280	f. 330 − 170 = _____

2. Use the arrow way to complete the number sentences. Use place value drawings if that will help you.

a.	b.	c.
$630 \xrightarrow{-400} \text{_____} \xrightarrow{+10} \text{_____}$	$570 \xrightarrow{-\_\_\_} 270 \xrightarrow{+\_\_\_} 290$	$\text{\_\_\_\_} \xrightarrow{-400} \text{\_\_\_\_} \xrightarrow{-40} 518$
630 − _____ = _____	570 − _____ = 290	_____ − 440 = 518

3. Solve.

Draw a place value chart with chips to model the problems. Show a written subtraction method to check your work.

---

a. 756 + 136

Subtraction Number Sentence:

---

b. 267 + 545

Subtraction Number Sentence:

Draw a place value chart with chips to model your work. Show a written addition method to check your work.

---

c. 617 – 229 = _____

Check:

---

d. 700 – 463 = _____

Check:

4. Find the missing numbers to make each statement true. Show your strategy to solve.

a. 300 – 106 = _____

b. _____ = 407 – 159

c. 410 – 190 = 420 - _____

d. 750 – 180 = _____ – 200

e. 900 – _____ = 600 – 426

5. Martha answered the problem 456 – 378 incorrectly. She does not understand her mistake.

    a.   Explain to Martha what she did wrong using place value language.

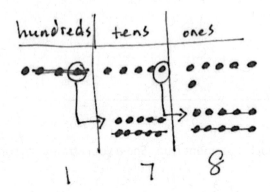

Explanation:

_____

_____

_____

    b.   Model an alternative strategy for 456 – 378 to help Martha avoid making this mistake again.

End-of-Module Assessment Task Standard Addressed	Topics A–D

Use Place Value Understanding and Properties of Operations to Add and Subtract

2.NBT.7 Add and subtract within 1000, using concrete models or drawings and strategies based on place value, properties of operations, and/or the relationship between addition and subtraction; relates the strategy to a written method. Understand that in adding and subtracting three-digit numbers, one adds or subtracts hundreds and hundreds, tens and tens, ones and ones; and sometimes it is necessary to compose or decompose tens or hundreds.

2.NBT.8 Mentally add 10 or 100 to a given number 100–900, and mentally subtract 10 or 100 from a given number 100–900.

2.NBT.9 Explain why addition and subtraction strategies work, using place value and the properties of operations. (Explanations may be supported by drawings or objects.)

Evaluating Student Learning Outcomes

A Progression Toward Mastery is provided to describe steps that illuminate the gradually increasing understandings that students develop *on their way to proficiency*. In this chart, this progress is presented from left (Step 1) to right (Step 4). The learning goal for each student is to achieve Step 4 mastery. These steps are meant to help teachers and students identify and celebrate what the student CAN do now and what they need to work on next.

A Progression Toward Mastery				
Assessment Task Item and Standards Assessed	STEP 1 Little evidence of reasoning without a correct answer. (1 Point)	STEP 2 Evidence of some reasoning without a correct answer. (2 Points)	STEP 3 Evidence of some reasoning with a correct answer or evidence of solid reasoning with an incorrect answer. (3 Points)	STEP 4 Evidence of solid reasoning with a correct answer. (4 Points)
1 2.NBT.7 2.NBT.8	The student solves one to two out of six parts correctly.	The student solves three to four to five out of six parts correctly.	The student solves five out of six parts correctly.	The student correctly shows a strategy to solve: a. 660 b. 565 c. 198 d. 50 e. 480 f. 160
2 2.NBT.7 2.NBT.8	The student solves zero out of three parts correctly.	The student solves one out of three parts correctly.	The student solves two out of three parts correctly.	The student correctly models the arrow way and solves to find: a. 230, 240, 390, 240 b. -300, +20, 280 c. 958, 558, 958
3 2.NBT.7 2.NBT.9	The student solves one out of four parts correctly.	The student solves two out of four parts correctly.	The student solves three out of four parts correctly.	The student correctly uses place value chips and writes a related subtraction method to solve: a. 892 b. 812 The student correctly uses place value chips and writes a related addition method to solve: c. 388 d. 237

A Progression Toward Mastery

4 2.NBT.7	The student answers one out of five parts correctly.	The student answers two to three out of five parts correctly.	The student answers four out of five parts correctly.	The student correctly shows a strategy to solve (strategies may vary): a. 194 b. 248 c. 200 d. 770 e. 726
5 2.NBT.7 2.NBT.9	The student answers zero out of two parts correctly.	The student answers one out of two parts correctly.	The student gives a partial explanation of Martha's error and correctly models an alternative strategy to solve, or the student gives an explanation of Martha's error and a partial model of an alternative strategy.	The student correctly: a. Explains that Martha made an error in the hundreds place while subtracting. b. Models an alternative strategy to solve.

Name **Kathy**   Date **Jan. 12**

1. Solve each problem with a written strategy such as: a tape diagram, number bond, the arrow way, the vertical method, or chips on a place value chart.

a. $460 + 200 = \underline{660}$ $460 \xrightarrow{+200} 660$	**b.** $\underline{565} = 865 - 300$ $865 \xrightarrow{-300} 565$	**c.** $\underline{198} + 400 = 598$ $\begin{array}{r} 598 \\ -400 \\ \hline 198 \end{array}$
d. $240 - 190 = \underline{50}$ 250 +10 240 +10 190 200 $250 - 200 = 50$	**e.** $\underline{480} = 760 - 280$ $760 \xrightarrow{-300} 460 \xrightarrow{+20} 480$	**f.** $330 - 170 = \underline{160}$ $330 \xrightarrow{-200} 130 \xrightarrow{+30} 160$

2. Use the arrow way to complete the number sentences. Use place value drawings if that will help you.

a. $630 \xrightarrow{-400} \underline{230} \xrightarrow{+10} \underline{240}$ $630 - \underline{390} = 240$	**b.** $570 \xrightarrow{-300} 270 \xrightarrow{+20} 290$ $570 - \underline{280} = 290$	**c.** $958 \xrightarrow{-400} \underline{558} \xrightarrow{-40} 518$ $\underline{958} - 440 = 518$

3. Solve:

Draw a place value chart with chips to model the problems. Show a written subtraction method to check your work.

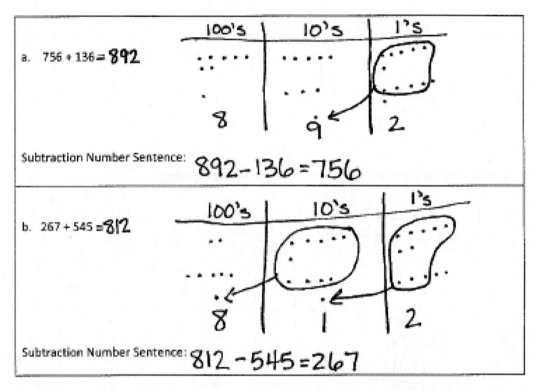

a. 756 + 136 = **892**

Subtraction Number Sentence: 892 – 136 = 756

b. 267 + 545 = **812**

Subtraction Number Sentence: 812 – 545 = 267

Draw a place value chart with chips to model your work. Show a written addition method to check your work.

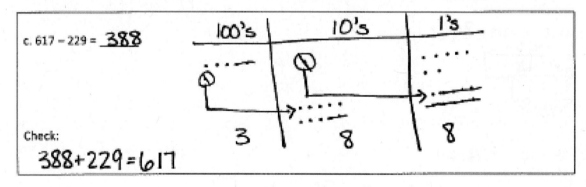

c. 617 – 229 = **388**

Check: 388 + 229 = 617

d. 700 – 463 = __237__

	100's	10's	1's

2   3   7

Check:

$237 + 463 = 700$

---

4. Find the missing numbers to make each statement true. Show your strategy to solve.

a. 300 – 106 = __194__

$$299$$
$$-105$$
$$\overline{194}$$

b. __248__ = 407 – 159

$$3\ 9\ 17$$
$$4\cancel{0}\cancel{7}$$
$$-1\ 5\ 9$$
$$\overline{248}$$

c. 410 – 190 = 420 - __200__

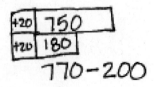

d. 750 – 180 = __770__ - 200

+20	750
+20	180

$770 - 200$

e. 900 - __726__ = 600 − 426

174

$$\begin{array}{r} 599 \\ -425 \\ \hline 174 \end{array}$$

$$\begin{array}{r} 899 \\ -173 \\ \hline 726 \end{array}$$

5. Martha answered the problem 400 − 378 incorrectly. She does not understand her mistake.

   a. Explain to Martha what she did wrong using place value language.

3 10 10

$$\begin{array}{r} 4\,0\,0 \\ -3\,7\,8 \\ \hline 3\,2 \end{array}$$

This should be a 9.

Explanation:

    Martha changed 1 hundred for 10 tens and 10 ones. It should have been changed for 9 tens and 10 ones.

   b. Model an alternate strategy for 400 − 378 to help Martha avoid making this mistake again.

Martha can take 1 from each number, then subtract.

$$\begin{array}{r} 399 \\ -377 \\ \hline 22 \end{array}$$